William Hanna Thomson

The Parables and their Home

The Parables by the Lake

William Hanna Thomson

The Parables and their Home
The Parables by the Lake

ISBN/EAN: 9783744762083

Printed in Europe, USA, Canada, Australia, Japan

Cover: Foto ©Lupo / pixelio.de

More available books at **www.hansebooks.com**

THE
PARABLES BY THE LAKE

BY

W. H. THOMSON, M.D., LL.D.

PROFESSOR OF MATERIA MEDICA AND DISEASES OF THE NERVOUS
SYSTEM, UNIVERSITY MEDICAL COLLEGE, N. Y.

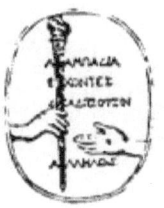

NEW YORK
HARPER & BROTHERS PUBLISHERS
1895

PREFACE

The Home of the Parables is a land which often affords striking commentaries of its own upon their meaning. To the writer of this volume, as the land of his birth and residence during youth, such aspects of the Parables naturally would be quite familiar. This fact accounts for the personal style adopted in the composition of these pages, as affording the simplest method in demonstrating the frequent relations of the Parables to the scenes and surroundings in which they were first delivered. It was intended to dedicate this volume to the writer's father, the Rev. William McClure Thomson, D.D., author of "The Land and the Book," a work widely known to the religious public, but before it was completed he was called this year to his rest.

New York, 7 Fifty-Sixth St. West.
December, 1894.

CONTENTS

	PAGE
THE SOWER .	1
THE SEED GROWING SECRETLY	43
THE TARES .	49
THE DRAW-NET	73
THE MUSTARD-SEED .	85
THE LEAVEN	101
THE HID TREASURE	. 117
THE PEARL .	. 133
THE HOUSEHOLDER'S TREASURE ..	. 145
CONCLUSION .	. 151

THE SOWER

Matt. xiii., 1–23.   Mark iv., 1–25.   Luke viii., 4–18.

The same day went Jesus out of the house, and sat by the sea-side. And great multitudes were gathered together unto him, so that he went into a ship, and sat; and the whole multitude stood on the shore. And he spake many things unto them in parables, saying, Behold, a sower went forth to sow; And when he sowed, some seeds fell by the way-side, and the fowls came and devoured them up: Some fell upon stony places, where they had not much earth: and forthwith they sprung up, because they had no deepness of earth: And when the sun was up [R. V. was risen], they were scorched; and because they had no root, they withered away. And some fell among thorns; and the thorns sprung up, and choked them: (Mark. And other fell on good ground, and did yield fruit that sprang up and increased; and brought forth, some thirty, and some sixty, and some a hundred.) Who hath ears to hear, let him hear.

And the disciples came, and said unto him, Why speakest thou unto them in parables? He answered and said unto them, Because it is given unto you to know the mysteries of the kingdom of heaven, but to them it is not given. For whosoever hath, to him shall be given, and he shall have more abundance: but whosoever hath not, from him shall be taken away even that he hath. Therefore speak I to them in parables: because they seeing, see not; and hearing, they hear not, neither do they understand. And unto them is fulfilled the prophecy of Isaiah, which saith,

> *By hearing ye shall hear, and shall in no wise understand;*
> *And seeing ye shall see, and shall in no wise perceive:*
> *For this people's heart is waxed gross,*
> *And their ears are dull of hearing,*
> *And their eyes they have closed;*
> *Lest haply they should perceive with their eyes,*
> *And hear with their ears,*
> *And understand with their heart,*
> *And should turn again,*
> *And I should heal them,*

(Mark. *And with many such parables spake he the word unto them, as they were able to hear it.*) *But blessed are your eyes, for they see: and your ears, for they hear. For verily I say unto you, That many prophets and righteous men have desired to see those things which ye see, and have not seen them, and to hear those things which ye hear, and have not heard them.*

Hear ye therefore the parable of the sower. When any one heareth the word of the kingdom, and understandeth it not, then cometh the wicked one, and catcheth away that which was sown in his heart. This is he which received seed by the way-side. But he that received the seed into stony places, the same is he that heareth the word, and anon with joy received it; Yet hath he not root in himself, but dureth for a while: for when tribulation or persecution ariseth because of the word, by and by [R.V. straightway] he is offended. He also that received seed among the thorns is he that heareth the word, and the care of this world, and the deceitfulness of riches, choke the word, and he becometh unfruitful. (Mark. *And the cares of this world, and the deceitfulness of riches, and the lusts of other things entering in, choke the word, and it becometh unfruitful.*) (Luke. *And that which fell among thorns are they which, when they have heard, go forth, and are choked with cares and riches and pleasures of this life, and bring no fruit to perfection.*) *But he that received seed into the good ground is he that heareth the word, and understandeth it; which also beareth fruit, and bringeth forth, some a hundredfold, some sixty, some thirty.* (Luke. *But that on the good ground are they, which in an honest and good heart, having heard the word, keep it [R.V. hold it fast], and bring forth fruit with patience.*)

THE SOWER

There is a form of deafness known to physicians in which the person affected is able to hear everything except words. In such a case the ear, as an apparatus for mere hearing, may be so perfect that the tick of a watch or the song of a bird is readily appreciated, but owing to a local injury deeper than the ear, for it is in the brain itself, all spoken words of his mother-tongue are as unintelligible to the sufferer as those of a foreign language. Give him a book, and he may read as understandingly as ever, but every word addressed to him through his ear reaches his consciousness only as a sound, not as a word.

There is a moral deafness which corresponds to this physical infirmity, but which, instead of being rare, is as common as it is harmful and disabling. To all men there is given an inner ear, which has been fashioned to hear wisdom's words, but that ear often seems so dull of hearing that there appears no sign of response to her utterances. Now it was just such an unreceptive state of soul and of feeling in the people which we are told led Jesus to speak to them in parables. But we cannot appreciate as we ought either the parables themselves, or the kind wisdom which led Jesus so to address that multitude by the lake, unless we first reproduce as faithfully as we can the human field on which the Teacher worked. In all problems of life the study of the subject of environment is not merely instructive, but is now recognized as an indispensable requisite; and in no case is this better illustrated than in the mental conditions with which our Saviour had then to deal.

Of the many causes of moral deafness, there was one which was especially operative in the first hearers of the parables, and that is, the interference of other ideas previously lodged in their minds. How small, therefore, would be the echo to the voice of spiritual truth in those inner chambers whose walls were hung thick with mistaken traditions, all embellished with the decorations of Oriental imagination, may be judged by the following considerations:

First, the multitude gathered to hear the "word of the kingdom" were already filled with thoughts instilled from childhood about the coming king. Any expected one must by so much be an ideal, and men's ideals are faithful reproductions of themselves in their hopes and wishes. Human imagination has no power to make pictures out of new materials, and hence every one of that Galilean throng brought with him an old and clearly defined picture of the promised Messiah, drawn in every detail from Eastern life and manners. The Messiah was to be a king, and to Orientals a king, first of all, must be formidable. To their minds he would not be a king at all if he were not personally dangerous even to friends. In the whole folk-lore of the East the kingly idiom is ever recognizable by its constant allusion to his power of ready slaying. Coupled with this would be a magnificence of state and of imposing retinue in which, for variety and true picturesqueness, the people of western Asia have excelled all other races. Neither European monarchs nor Chinese emperors, owing to defects in costume, have ever equalled the spectacular effects of royal processions among the Shemitic peoples. A Jewish Solomon or an Arab Haroun-al-Raschid could ride arrayed and adorned as no other mode of dress allows for both grace and splendor, and at the same time for suggesting the king's immeasurable elevation above all other men. I have seen Arab dignitaries riding, not at the head of, but, better, surrounded by, a great cavalcade of attendants, with scarcely two of them arrayed alike, and yet without a single artistic incongruity in the whole company to mar the effect or to lessen the impression of the scene; so much does the Oriental dress allow of variety with harmony, both in form and color. We may be sure, therefore, that of the thousands at the lake that day, not one, from the rabbi to the peasant, but hoped to live to hail the Messiah's coming in just such outward fulfilment of the prophetic psalm, "Gird thy sword upon thy thigh, O Mighty One! And in thy majesty ride on prosperously" (Psalm xlv. 3, 4).

Hence came another conception inseparable from such an ideal. A king and a warrior are words anciently coupled everywhere, familiar enough in European literature itself of but a century ago. But no nation could have longed more naturally for a warrior king than the Jews of that day. The heroic figure of Judas Maccabæus rose to every mind as a promise of the mightier Son of David coming fitly against a mightier oppressor than Antiochus. A greater than Cæsar would be here. Whose heart, indeed, would not burn, even among ourselves now, at the thought of the avenger of that one scene alone, though there were many others like it, which but a few years before was enacted by the proconsul Varus, when he crucified two thousand of its chosen youths in groups at all the cross-roads of the land as a demonstration of what Rome was to them?

The King, indeed, had come, but how could he be recognized in him who was sitting in a poor fisherman's boat?—he who was known as a carpenter and the son of a carpenter, belonging, therefore, to the poorest craft in a land where carpenters have less to do than in any settled country. This is not alone from the scarcity and poor quality of its lumber, but because in their stone houses the people have little need for carpenters except to make one rough door and one or two windows. At this day one may admire the elegant stone architecture of the houses of the rich in Syrian cities, and yet note in them the cheap rudeness of all carpenter-work. But though his own personality might not have been disappointing, the same could not be said of his body attendants. Dress among Orientals is an immediate and unmistakable mark of rank, and even of intellectual grade. The scribe and the rabbi had their full-dress, just as no one now mistakes the dignified figure of the Moslem ulem. But the chosen companions of Jesus belonged to the only class in the country below dress, as they were so commonly seen at their daily labor without it. It is one of those conclusive incidental references which stamp as genuine the last written words of the New Testament,* where, though by that

---

* A chronological arrangement of the New Testament ac-

time Christians had become throughout the world, and according to Tacitus even in Rome itself, "a vast multitude," and were found in Cæsar's palace, yet John does not shrink from representing Peter, after the Resurrection, returning to do his work as of old, naked. (John xxi. 7.) Neither was it repellent to the rich alone that Jesus surrounded himself with pariahs. The peasants of Palestine still have a pride in the show of their superiors, and would resent the promotion from their own ranks of such as Salome's two sons, who looked forward to the vizier's seats on the right and left

---

cording to the date of composition of its separate books would begin with the First Epistle to the Thessalonians, and would end with the writings of St. John, who, according to the universal tradition, survived its other authors. The general opinion of scholars is that Revelation was written some twenty years before the Fourth Gospel, and from the time of Tertullian chapter xxi. has been commonly regarded as a postscript to the Gospel, which otherwise would end with the 29th verse of chapter xx. It is supposed that the 21st chapter was added by the apostle to correct a mistaken report (vs. 23) current in the Christian community that our Lord had said that John should not die. From vs. 19 it is plain that St. Peter was already dead.

hand of the king when at last he would put off his disguise.

That such were the conceptions of the multitude, as they stood waiting to hear about the kingdom, we know from the apostles themselves. Whatever else they were, sincere and good men they show that they were by their uniformly humble estimate of themselves. In their memoirs of their Master, out of some twenty-eight allusions to something which they either said or did, twenty-six are to their discredit. Hence they tell us that not all their close personal intercourse with Jesus himself sufficed to displace from their minds their native ideal of the Messiah's advent. Whoever, therefore, understands human nature, can discern that one miracle at least occurred at Pentecost, when those same men so suddenly showed that they knew at last what the Kingdom of the Parables truly was. Before that day not even the mighty impression of the Resurrection had kept them from asking, "Lord, dost thou at this time restore the kingdom to Israel?" (Acts i. 6)—a most natural question in the world in their then mental state, while it impressively illustrates the words of their Master on the way to Gethsemane, "I have yet many things to say unto you, but ye cannot bear them now. Howbeit when He, the Spirit of Truth is come, he shall guide you into all the truth" (John xvii. 12, 13).

Jesus, therefore, spoke now to the multitude in parables because he knew what was in men. Not an idea from outside could penetrate the dense thickets of their mental prepossessions, and therefore only a thought working from within could have any chance of a recognition. That a parable alone could accomplish. For such as he was to utter a parable they all knew meant much. Not only by his own preaching, but by that of John the Baptist, the whole nation had been stirred up with the announcement that the kingdom of heaven was at hand. They clearly recognized in Jesus a greater than a rabbi, even a great prophet at least, and great prophets were wont to speak just thus. Simply as Orientals they could appreciate a speaker in parables, for Orientals are rarely orators. Their wise men do not rise to speak, but rather sit and deliver their message as a father instructs his child. A formal prologue or an eloquent peroration in such case would be wholly out of place. Therefore, soon as they found that Jesus was speaking to them in parables, the multitude was awe-struck. So spake the seers of old to their fathers. At once they knew that the responsibility was on them to divine what he meant about the kingdom. A late distinguished medical teacher (Sir Andrew Clark) said, "The criterion of true instruction is not acquiring, but thinking." Judged by that criterion, the witness of the ages is that never man spake as did Jesus then in thought-awakening words, when he spoke to them in parables.

Some commentators have strangely misunderstood our Lord's answer to the question of the disciples why he spoke thus to the multitude, as implying that it was to conceal his teaching from them as a judicial punishment for the state of mind they were in, while privately he explained the truth to his followers because only to them was the privilege vouchsafed of entering into the mysteries of the kingdom of heaven. But we may be sure that

Christ never chose such a form of judgment for sin, and that he who said at this time "there is nothing hid that shall not be made manifest" (Mark iv. 22), scarcely would himself form a secret order of the initiated among men. On the contrary, our Lord's words, illustrated by the apt quotation from Isaiah, are simply descriptive of the mental state of the multitude, a state which precluded any appreciation of spiritual truth by them in comparison with his more enlightened disciples. Hence as one would begin to teach unlettered nomads or savages how to read by pictures or object-lessons, so Jesus chose the parable, first, to fix the attention, and then to awaken inquiry among men, dwelling as they were in the thick shadow of Galilean darkness. Much more favored are those who can learn without pictures, for with them progress in knowledge is both easier and cumulative. His disciples, therefore, could begin to grasp the explanation of the parable when he gave it to them, while the man of the multitude knew that it had a meaning too deep for him then, but offered to him to search out as he caught the impressive refrain, "He who hath ears to hear, let him hear!" This fact at least about the parable the man of the multitude well knew by his birth, for Orientals peculiarly appreciate metaphors, and expect it whenever profound truths are the theme of the teacher.

A word about the scene. I have heard of travellers being disappointed with their first view of the Lake of Tiberias, but I have always regarded it as analogous to the feelings of many persons when they first look upon a picture by one of the old masters. One needs to look upon the Sea of Galilee often and long to appreciate its singular beauty. Accustomed as we are, Americans especially, to heavily wooded landscapes, the rocky, treeless mountains all about the lake except where separated from it by the bare plain of Gennesaret, seem a picture of general desolation. Ere long, however, the varied features of steep slopes, gorges, precipices, and successive bold indentations of the shores, are seen to form a splendid setting for the deep blue waters of the lake itself. But as the sun declines, tints of so many exquisite hues come out in the landscape that the eye grows bewildered with the ceaseless variety of its enjoyments. Among the many visits which I have made to the lake, there was one which gave us a sudden view of it as we emerged from the long valley which is given in Joshua xix. as belonging to the tribe of Naphtali. We had followed this yet olive-planted vale as it runs east from the plain of Acre, and just before sunset found it opening on the basin of Tiberias, with the ruined site of Capernaum far below. A peculiarly serene quiet rested upon the whole scene, every line of which showed through the transparent air, from the flashing snow of Hermon on the north to the exit of the Jordan on the south, with mountain, plain, and lake bathed in colors which suggested the thought that John drew from his native memories the materials for the glorious dream of the jewelled city descending from the heaven.

We must remember, however, that in our Saviour's time all the mountain-sides were green with vineyard terraces, or rose in steps for thousands of feet of olive orchards, with villages embowered among fig and almond trees on every slope, while turreted castles and walled cities crowned the precipices all around the lake. Of the fertility and populousness of the plain of Gennesaret, Josephus (*Bell.* iii. 10, 7) gives us a glowing account, and we may be sure that it presented a picture equal to that of the Damascus plain now, with here many a palm grove and tropical beauty that would make the contrast of the whole scene with its present waste as marked as the change would be to the most beautiful face of woman if her hair were completely shorn.

The soil of Galilee is remarkable for its possession of a guarantee for enduring fertility in the nature of its rock, which is a limestone so abounding in shells and animal remains that its disintegration by the heavy winter rains is constantly re-enriching it. The most vigorous growth of wheat may therefore be seen on land which at first sight seems covered with stones. A field in America, with the soil in one part so thin over rock that no seed can mature, could scarcely promise sixty or a hundred fold elsewhere in it. But not so here, where the heaviest crops are gathered from immediate proximity to bare rock itself. As the table-land on the west breaks down into the volcanic depression of the Jordan valley, the rich lava loam is mixed with the washings of the limestone hills, with the effect of producing that exceptional fertility of which Josephus so proudly speaks.

The first winter rains cause the earth to break forth into a wealth of flowers, which continue to increase until in spring this beauteous coat of many colors completely covers the surface. Their variety of form and color also baffles description. A French botanist, who had a commission from the Jardin des Plantes of Paris, told me that after five years of collecting in Syria he seemed as far as ever from completing his work; and that though he had visited Buenos Ayres, the Cape of Good Hope, and the Moluccas, yet he had found no land which could compare with Syria for its flowers. It is here also that the Huleh lily, which surpasses in loveliness all lilies of the field, has its native home. One has but to look at it to see how vain it would be for man to imitate its glory.

We are thus brought at the outset to one of those spiritual parallels in the life of man which appear with such inexplicable naturalness whenever the parables make us think, that we seem led to ask, was not this visible world, after all, created from the beginning to be man's great parable? The sower went forth to sow, but he had been there before! He does not begin to sow until after he has broken the ground all up. But how many flowers he ruins in doing this! So many a man and woman can say that their field was once filled with nature's fairest attractions, until the Sower came and buried all, not excepting, perhaps, that matchless lily, which we would think he could have spared. Certainly at first nothing could seem more desolating work than his, or anything less likely than that the field will ever regain its former joyous face. Even when it will best answer his purpose, and wave with his seed-bearing growth, it will not then appear as bright as when it was gay with its former robe. Nevertheless, all experience tells us that it is just when life seems all broken up by upheavals which the man neither caused nor could prevent, and when human consolation, therefore, is impotent, because it knows not what to say, that the human heart is oftener ready to receive the seed of the kingdom than ever before.

The divisions of land are still the same in Palestine as in Bible times. No fences separate one man's field from another's, the division being the eye line between tall stones erected as landmarks. In comparison with our stiffly enclosed meadows, this much enhances the park-like effect of a plain when green with wheat, while it recalls many a passage of the Old Testament against the wicked who remove a neighbor's landmark, a form of robbery of the weak by the strong still known in this country. The roads, or rather the bridle-paths which go for roads, are so narrow as they pass through the fields that every sower has to cast some of the seed on the wayside for the fowls of the air to pick up. Birds in Syria, and especially about the Lake of Tiberias, are extraordinarily numerous. Some twelve miles above Tiberias is the first lake of the Jordan, or the Waters of Merom of the

Bible, at the end of the rich plain now called the Huleh, but which plain becomes a vast marsh ere it merges into that lake. As Syria is the winter feeding-ground of many migratory birds from Northern Europe and Asia, this marsh is then filled with a greater variety and multitude of waterfowl than I have ever seen elsewhere. But towards evening its extensive canebrakes resound with the noise of myriads of crows, which come from all quarters of the heavens to its secure resting-place. At early dawn they begin their calls again, and then make long lines of flight for the nearest wheat-fields. As once we were descending to the plain of Gennesaret, we passed a hill-side which was black with over a thousand of them, who were waiting there for the unhappy ploughmen to move far enough away for them to descend on their fields. In addition to the crows, there are great flocks also of the rock-pigeons who live in the many precipices above the lake. As I tried to shoot some of them, I noticed that when they rose in their powerful flight they never stopped short of their lofty hiding-places ere they lit, though in a short time they would swoop down to the plain again. "How say ye to my soul, flee as a bird to your mountain," said the psalmist.

Modern physiology of the nervous system has its lessons about the application of this part of the parable. According to the laws of reflex association, it is plain that much the greater number of our ideas are not self-generated at all, but are simple reflex responses to the impressions coming to us from the outer world through our senses. Our brain is a thinking machine in which thoughts arise in response to every variety of external suggestion, and in numbers as countless as the birds of the air which come from north, south, east, and west on a field in Gennesaret to catch away the seed of the sower. We are not responsible for the thoughts which enter our minds. No man ever was. What we are responsible for is for the thoughts which we allow to stay there, because we have a kingly centric power within us which can compel this mechanically thinking brain to do its thinking at its behest. The will, by its lawful, physiological, inhibitory power, can say to the thinking brain, these thoughts are good and valuable seed-thoughts, therefore keep them; those thoughts are purposeless and hence unprofitable, therefore dismiss them at once, and a well-disciplined mind will obey. Now each step in the parable of the sower is from the weaker men to the stronger. The weakest of all are those characterized habitually with flying thoughts. It is a feeble, often a diseased, mind which thinks hurriedly. Let a man be reduced by a fever or other cause of exhaustion, and he has hard work to keep his mental machine from turning out thoughts that run to the ends of the earth. A rapid flow of ideas, indeed, is often the sign of impending mental ruin, as in the approach of maniacal insanity. Deep thought, on the other hand, implies prolonged thought, and no mental machine can think long and well on one subject unless it has learned the weary lesson of thinking by will. But in the ordinary world of men, how rare is the man who has that most precious of all possessions—self-possession, so that he can compel his mind to dismiss its many birds of the air whenever he chooses. Instead of that with many scarce has a good seed-thought time to fall upon their uncultivated soil ere it is quickly displaced by flitting ideas from the farthest horizon. Our Saviour says that Satan comes quickly to the wayside hearer and catches away the seed; but Satan, like every other spiritual agency, has to work through our natural laws of mental suggestion. That he can best do by promoting mental desultoriness, for those are swayed easiest who have the least control over their own thinking. For seed to germinate into serious or settled purpose it must have more time than the wayside weakling ever gives to anything.

The shallow soil of the next class receives the seed long enough to have it germinate, and indeed to be greener than the rest of the field for a time. It is a mistake, however, to confound this class with impulsive characters in general. Persons of an impulsive temperament are often so on account of a naturally strong warmth of feeling, and thus they may be among the best and sweetest persons in the world. Their many mishaps, however, often cause them to be underrated, as inferior to really smaller natures with cooler heads. But it should be remembered that He who never mistook men, from the first called the impulsive and oft-stumbling Peter, the Rock (John i. 42).

The stony-ground hearers, on the other hand, are that numerous class who in any new thing see only its favorable aspects, and sanguinely follow, expecting nothing else. But it takes a deeper nature than theirs to weigh the difficulties which come with all true good in life. Hence they are too weak in soul to encounter difficulties, and with the first experience thereof, as Mark expresses it (R.V.), "having no root in themselves, straightway they stumble and fall before it."

No part of the parable of the sower derives so much illustration from the land in which it was first uttered as that which tells of the seed and the thorns. These thorns are not brier-bushes or brambles among which the seed falls, but an after-growth of a variety of thistles, as is intimated in the phrase, "the thorns sprang up and choked it." These thistles come up thickly in every wheat-field in Palestine, but the natural time for them to appear is after the wheat is ripened. When, therefore, the wheat is reaped the ground is seen covered with the new green growth of this strong-leaved thistle, which then springs rapidly up to about the same height, and as dense, as the wheat which preceded it. As it dries it becomes very hard, with a metallic ring when struck, and turns white, so that at a distance it resembles a harvest-field with grain, and thus gives point to the words of Jeremiah (xii. 13), "They have sown wheat, but shall reap thorns"—a very painful harvest, for the spikes on the thistles' leaves are both long and sharp. But as the productive parts of a field in Palestine will sooner or later be covered with these thorns, the lesson of the parable is not that Christians will escape thorny days by rich fruit-bearing. Strong and abundant thistles, on the contrary, are signs of naturally good soil. It is Christian to be diligent in business, though the result be increase in the world's goods, with consequent cares and responsibilities. But what a sower in Palestine knows that he should do is to get his seed in early. If he sows too late, his wheat will then have a hard contest with the inevitable thorns which will be sure to appear in their time. Sometimes, however, late sowing in Palestine cannot be helped, because the "early rain" of Scripture, which ought to fall in the last week of September, has been delayed. After the dry season which follows the "latter rain" in May, the autumn showers are needful to soften the earth enough for the Syrian farmer, with his rude wooden plough, to break the soil up. When this rain is missed, the peasants are often obliged to band together, so that a number of them may be seen following each other in the same furrow to make it deep enough; a fact which explains the passage in 1 Kings xix. 19, where, after the three years' drought, Elijah first meets Elisha ploughing with twelve yoke of oxen, Elisha being with the twelfth. With such slow ploughing, however, parts of the field are sown much earlier than other parts; the last, therefore, having a future before it of, at best, mixed wheat and thistles.

This portion of the parable, therefore, adverts to the grave spiritual dangers of middle life. Get the heavenly seed in early; for if it be first received in the time that the cares of this life are multiplying, it is the nature of these to grow, after they start, much faster than wheat ever does. This world's possessions, when won, can be kept only by being constantly watched; but the men are few who can be deeply interested at the same time with quite diverse objects. Gradually the earlier and better seed languishes and declines, while a change of interest unconsciously goes on, which is daily ministered to by family, friends, and associates. I have seen some good stalks of wheat which have managed to hold their own against the crowd of thistles all around them; but in the field of life, those who would approach Christians in such case are apt to feel the prick of the thorns sooner than they can recognize the Sower's fruit, so hedged in are they likely to be with the hard exclusiveness of worldly prosperity. The usual result, however, of a life filled with this world's interests is that nothing is grown for the future. A seed of wheat, though the product of this season, yet contains assurance of next year's growth. If it stopped short of that it would not be fruit. So Christian fruit will be shown to be fruit for the next world when the angels gather the harvest. They, no more than earthly reapers, will take the seed which has no germ for the future, because it has spent itself here.

The deceptive resemblance at a distance of a thistle-covered field to one of good grain has its counterpart in many a showy but utterly barren, if not cruel, growth of modern civilization. The passion for mere material success is the snare of our time, which threatens to dwarf every kind of good seed in literature and art as well as in religion, for the deceitfulness of richness may delude an age quite as certainly as an individual. With an individual, however, it is pitiable to see how all the world combines to deceive the rich man about himself by its show of deference to his every word, as if he gave the weight to his gold instead of his gold to him. The effect of this misinterpreted verdict of his fellows is to engender in the man that most complete of all deceptions, the self-deception of the self-satisfied.

Also, in the Church at large, there often come times of spiritual drought, when the whole field seems overrun with earth's thistles. The oft-given promise of the Old Testament, "I will pour out my Spirit upon you," suggested to Palestinians the anxiously hoped for "early rain," which enables the sower to go forth to sow as soon as the long summer drought is broken. So when in the Church these gracious seasons are much delayed, we need not be surprised at the marked growth of worldliness, with its painful thorns, when only the bread of life should be found.

It is, however, at the parable's closing words about the seed which fell on good ground that our Lord sought to have each ear fully awakened to hear. Instead of those failures whose sadness will be fully known only when the kingdom is come in heaven, we have now the conditions of that success which will be the joy of the Great Harvest. He explained that the fruit-yielding hearers are those who both "receive" the word into their hearts and then "keep" it there. To receive here means to appreciate, and appreciation is a weighty word! It testifies to a power of estimating values or aims in life which is possible only to a richly endowed being like man. Often the possession of this power, or the lack of it, at a particular juncture, determines a man's destiny thereafter. How generally, from the lack of it, does sin itself come, because rarely does one commit a sin with any appreciation at the time of what he is doing. Likewise opportunities lost are simply opportunities not appreciated. Wisdom itself may be defined as the timely appreciation of the relative importance of things, and acting accordingly. Hence wisdom is always selective, but on that very account implies the possession of strength, for amid the many attractions in human life it takes a strong nature so to appreciate the better thoughts when they come that they will be kept until they take deep root, a result which can follow only upon much and prolonged effort, or, as the revised version expresses it (Luke viii. 15), they "hold it fast and bring forth fruit with patience."

Unlike most physical or chemical processes, growth requires much time, and good seed especially must be long retained and carefully cultivated. Hence the failures with the preceding classes were that each in its own way failed to "keep" what the sower gave. The wayside hearer never began to appreciate it; both the other two received, but failed to keep, thus showing that good thoughts should be reverted to again and again, or they will die out. Scarcely any figure, therefore, could describe so aptly as this parable does the common human experience with good thoughts. We all have our times when good thoughts come into our minds as seed falls gently from a sower's hand. Often their excellence is then recognized, and we feel that a good moment is upon us, with suggestions of a better life to be begun by us anew. Yet how soon we find the appreciation of them grow less and less, until finally the thoughts themselves die out! But we should remember that no good thoughts ever make us better until they have become habitual. Only when they have become that have they taken root, for thoughts influence life and conduct not by their impressiveness, but by their permanence.

But scarcely any one can look over his mental field without finding it occupied with many an old mental weed which has for long been exhausting its soil. The decision must then be made whether the good seed, which can always be had of the Heavenly Sower for the asking, shall be not only sown, but then carefully attended to. If it be so kept, the weeds will be killed out, for the two are mutually exclusive of each other. The longer the good seed grows the stronger it grows, according to the law of verse 12, "Whosoever hath, to him it shall be given, and he shall have abundance." The power of appreciating the relative worth of things grows with its exercise. Good thoughts already retained make the retention of others like them easier. More and more seed then will be sown in time, for it is only over poor ground that the sower passes but once, while he returns again and again to the more promising soil to make sure that it gets its full share.

While some may not agree with Buffon that

genius is patience, yet none will deny that true patience always implies strength of character. It is far from being mere endurance. There is no such thing as a patient ox; for, though animals may be passive at labor, they cannot be patient, because patience demands a purposive as well as continuous self-restraint. Therefore, instead of being a passive quality, its exercise calls for activity of the highest order. It needs power to maintain that mastery which will prevent strength from being wasted by yielding to impulses and inclinations. It is instructive, therefore, to note how physiology abounds with illustrations of the place which the great law of control has in all sentient life. Thus the heart is supplied with two opposing sets of nerves. If one be stimulated by an electrical current it causes the heart to beat rapidly. Stimulation of the other filament causes the heart to beat slowly. Now if this latter nerve be cut, the heart at once bounds off into a tumultuous rapid action, behaving like a horse which has thrown his rider. Throughout the nervous system, indeed, we have constant examples of similar restraining arrangements of nerves and of nerve-centres which are technically said to "inhibit" the action of other nerves or nerve-centres, and the view is now held that this inhibiting function is for the special purpose of conserving and of regulating energy. That man has a strong heart whose pulse remains steady when evil tidings suddenly come; while he whose heart beats violently at a small provocation not only has his cardiac inhibiting nerve weak, but he is likely to be weak throughout, from lack of that reserve power without which no one can be patient. Therefore as, in the material living world, fruit-bearing is not only the slowest and the last product of growth, but also that which makes the greatest demand on vitality, so, in the moral world, none but the strong in spirit do so " possess their souls in patience " that they fail not in the long, silent process of bringing forth fruit to perfection.

In this parable, while the soil corresponds to the human, the seed corresponds to the Divine element in the sowing. Now it is in a seed that the whole mystery of life on earth is enwrapped. This mystery modern science has intensified far beyond what men in the age of the parables could have imagined. Then men thought that what they saw in a seed of wheat, or in an acorn, was the first beginning of the great after-growth. We now know that the actually living part of such seeds is wonderfully smaller, and, in fact, at first is to the unaided eye invisibly hid in the mass of the apparent seed, for this consists mainly of a store of food for the true seed within when it shall begin to grow. It is, therefore, at a seed that all who attempt materialistic explanations of life find themselves baffled. Every living thing, be it an oak or a whale, has to begin its individual existence as a unicellular organism, a microscopic speck. To the biologist, therefore, it is a much greater thing when it exists as a vanishing-point of matter, than when it has attained to the vast bulk of mature development, for by that time it has outgrown and spent many of the potencies which were in it at the beginning. In that small beginning not only was every after-development already determined to a finality, but it also contained the stored-up inheritance of untold generations.

It is in view of such facts that one of the chief physical philosophers of our day, Lord Kelvin, says, "The growth of generation after generation of plants from a single seed is infinitely different from any possible results of the fortuitous concourse of atoms. The real phenomena of life infinitely transcend human science." *

So we may say of the seed of the Word of the Kingdom, there is in it a mystery which the world constantly fails to recognize. Constantly it mistakes Christ the Sower as only a great teacher of morals, or, as technically termed, ethics. But Christ did not come to teach ethics. The world did not need him for that. The world was not then, nor has it ever been, in want of men who could say all that need be said about morals, that is, about how men should behave to each other. Egyptian epitaphs show that for more than thirty centuries before Christ men had very clear ideas about good behavior. In Christ's time,

---

* Sir William Thomson, now Lord Kelvin, President of the Royal Society. Article in the *Fortnightly Review*, March, 1892.

also, the writings of Jewish rabbis and of Greek and Roman philosophers did abound with unexceptionable ethics, and yet their world was perishing from soul starvation all the same. Seneca, the wealthy and cultivated Roman, wrote a book of moral maxims which is admired for its excellence to this day; but of the effects of his teaching he gave the world two instructive illustrations: first in his favorite pupil Nero, and secondly in himself, when, notwithstanding all his ethics, he shocked even Rome by rising in the Senate to justify the revolting murder by Nero of his own mother.

No; there is a fundamental difference between the seed of the parable and ethics. Ethics speaks only of a perfected earthly life; a life, therefore, which, however ethical, must end, like any other earthly life, in death. Christ here tells of life in the kingdom of heaven. Now, ethics is no more religion than geometry is astronomy. It is true that we must begin with accurate geometry before we can begin to estimate the relations to us in space of the heavenly bodies, and so righteousness in our earthly lives is an indispensable prerequisite for the life beyond. But mere ethics is as much restricted to this life as mere geometry, or earth measuring, is to this earth. Therefore, to regard the sower of this parable as only another teacher of old ethics, is as mistaken as the view that a seed of wheat consists only of certain physical substances which are nutritious; but were it not for the living thing within it, the seed would not contain one of those life-sustaining principles. It is true that the world as naturally demands that the Christian should be an example of good morals, as that wheat should be good for food. There is no such thing as a Christian life without good deeds, any more than a living germ of wheat without its rich enwrapping. The one form of life can no more begin to grow without its essential accompaniment than the other. But the true Christian receives from the Prince of Life much more than good morals—nothing less than the gift of life in distinction from death. What, in fact, can mere ethics do against death? Will moral discourse, for example, bind up the broken heart after the entrance of death into one's house? Death is wholly impartial on all questions about morals: the good and the evil die alike. How, therefore, can ethics console human grief on account of death? It is in the tidings about the kingdom alone that we hear anything worth hearing about death and life. Christ is our life from now on, because he has changed death into sleep, which therefore has an awakening, when he shall bring us back to our Father, to see God face to face. He who has this hope will seek, indeed, to purify himself as his heart is stirred within him by an incentive which no mere ethics, with its earthly limitations, could ever supply.

No one can conclude his meditations on the lessons of this parable without becoming sensible of a certain peculiar elevation in it above human ideals, for which there is no explanation on natural or historical principles. His auditors were eager above everything else to hear about the kingdom, and Jesus likens it to what no one, either before or after, likened a kingdom—to seed growing in some individual hearts until it bears fruit there of its own heavenly kind. But we need not wonder that such a conception would hardly suggest to that Jewish multitude a reference to the kingdom of their expected Son of David. This lesson was equally lost upon men who were not Jews, for we find it still far above Christian thought for many centuries afterwards. Strictly parallel to the Jewish idea of the Israel of God, there arose among Christians the conception of the Church of God as the kingdom of heaven on earth. But no sooner did the Church win the sword of the Cæsars, as the Jews had hoped that the Messiah would do for them, than all thought of the kingdom as a source of life in the heart gave place to the old ante-Pentecostal dreams of James and John and Salome. To the minds of such good men as St. Augustine and St. Jerome the earthly king was to be the Church's king also. Augustine urged Count Boniface to hang and every way to persecute the Donatists, saying of the text, "Blessed are ye who suffer for righteousness' sake," that they are equally blessed who inflict persecution for the sake of righteousness! Jerome in similar vein said, "Cruelty in God's cause is not impiety!" Such misconceptions of the kingdom not only silenced the Gospel to unconverted nations for more than a thousand years, but filled Christendom itself with blood, and rent the body of Christ into many hostile divisions. Against fatal perversions like these there can be no better corrective than to revert to this first Word of the Kingdom, which speaks of its being a silent inner principle of life direct from the hand of the Lord from heaven, and which, in contrast with the thoughts of men, is like passing from the desolate shores of the Dead Sea and its bitter waters, to the sweet scenes of the peaceful Lake of Galilee.

THE SEED GROWING SECRETLY

Mark iv., 26-29.

And he said, So is the kingdom of God, as if a man should cast seed into the ground; And should sleep, and rise night and day, and the seed should spring and grow up, he knoweth not how. For the earth bringeth forth fruit of herself; first the blade, then the ear, after that the full corn in the ear. But when the fruit is brought forth, immediately he putteth in the sickle, because the harvest is come.

THE SEED GROWING SECRETLY

Another association by our Lord of the kingdom with the life in a seed is given by St. Mark (iv. 26-29) as following upon the parable of the sower, in the words, "And he said, So is the kingdom of God, as if a man should cast seed into the ground; and should sleep, and rise night and day, and the seed should spring and grow up, he knoweth not how. For the earth bringeth forth fruit of herself; first the blade, then the ear, after that the full corn in the ear. But when the fruit is brought forth, immediately he putteth in the sickle, because the harvest is come."

The main instruction of this passage is that the kingdom of God cometh not with observation, because it is essentially a life within, and life's manifestations can only be seen, not known. Thus, as we have already noted, all the watchful observation and experiment of modern science have failed to find the slightest explanation of what the life in a seed is. Still it grows, while no man knoweth either how it begins to grow, or how it grows from the blade to the ear, and then on till it is ready for the sickle. In like manner the kingdom has appeared in the story of the world and in the experience of individuals. The philosophy of history is a sounding term, applied to attempts to trace the laws and the causes of historical developments according to certain natural principles. Climate, geographical position, race, customs, institutions, and, finally, events and persons, are thus supposed both to make and to explain history. But the Church of Christ in history refuses to be explained by any or by all of these things, for time shows that she has been wholly independent of them. While in secular history the successive steps may be observed, just as in the erection of a building we can watch each stone as it is added to the rest, the story of the Church is that of a living growth which develops by the hidden power within itself operating unceasingly day and night. Each age, as it has been occupied with its own passing concerns, has been as little conscious of the silent progress of the kingdom as the husbandman is able to note by the hour how his grain is growing. But as we look back over the centuries, and see through how many different phases of inner conflict and of external danger the Church of Christ has passed, and has left them all behind, we may well say that the "how" of that marvellous continuity through so many changes we know not. What we can see is that it means life.

This parable was given for our encouragement as well as for our instruction. The depression of many Christians in face of the opposing forces of their times, or on account of what they imagine to be the slow progress of the kingdom in the world, is largely due to the difficulty of watching a living growth at all. Growth often goes on even more rapidly in the silent night than by day. The times of one generation as little suffice to measure the advance of the kingdom as the hours of one day suffice to show how rapidly the crop is growing which takes a whole season to mature. On some cold and overcast days it may appear scarcely to grow at all. So it seemed throughout Christendom at the close of the last century. But the seed still lives through cold and dark days, and in due time it will yield its golden harvest.

With many individual Christians also the subject of their spiritual growth is too often one of anxiety, because they cannot recognize its daily increase. The best cure for this morbid introspection is for the man to go about his Master's business, as the man in the parable did about his, and let the seed alone, for he cannot tell either how it grows or when it is growing most. To be constantly inspecting the seed to discover whether it be taking deep root or not, is as poor husbandry in the spiritual as in the material field. He who gave the seed at the beginning is not only the Author, but the Finisher of our faith.

THE TARES

Matt. xiii., 24-30; 36-43.

Another parable put he forth unto them, saying, The kingdom of heaven is likened unto a man which sowed good seed in his field: But while men slept, his enemy came and sowed tares [R.V. also] among the wheat, and went his way. But when the blade was sprung up, and brought forth fruit, then appeared the tares also. So the servants of the householder came and said unto him, Sir, didst not thou sow good seed in thy field? from whence then hath it tares? He said unto them, An enemy hath done this. The servant said unto him, Wilt thou then that we go and gather them up? But he said, Nay; lest while ye gather up the tares, ye root up also the wheat with them. Let both grow together until the harvest; and in the time of harvest I will say to the reapers, Gather ye together first the tares, and bind them in bundles to burn them: but gather the wheat into my barn.

Then Jesus sent the multitude away, and went into the house: and his disciples came unto him, saying, Declare unto us the parable of the tares of the field. He answered and said unto them, He that soweth the good seed is the Son of man; The field is the world; the good seed are the children of the kingdom; but the tares are the children of the wicked one; The enemy that sowed them is the devil; the harvest is the end of the world; and the reapers are the angels. As therefore the tares are gathered and burned in the fire; so shall it be in the end of this world. The Son of man shall send forth his angels, and they shall gather out of his kingdom all things that offend, and them which do iniquity; And shall cast them into a furnace of fire: there shall be wailing and gnashing of teeth. Then shall the righteous shine forth as the sun in the kingdom of their Father. Who hath ears to hear, let him hear.

THE TARES

FULLY as familiar to the people's ears as the mention of a sower going forth to sow, would be the reference to the tares of the field. So well did they know just what tares are for trouble, annoyance, and injury, that to hear of something parallel to them as inseparably associated with their expected kingdom must have bewildered them with surprise and disappointment. They could not possibly give a pleasant interpretation to such a presage of the future, nor could they minimize its unwelcome import. When the wheat first clothes the field with its green mantle, there is little to suggest to the Palestinian farmer any fear that his toil will fail of the reward of a good harvest. The mildew and the insect enemies which so commonly ruin wheat in America are there comparatively rare, and he simply prays that the "latter rain" will fall in its due season to bring out the ears of wheat to their rich, full size.

But as the time for the heading out of the wheat approaches, he watches anxiously to see whether a disguised enemy has not been all along growing in the midst of the wheat, unperceived on account of a close resemblance to it whilst in the blade. By the fruit he soon recognizes whether this be so or not. There can be no mistake then. As once I heard it remarked in that country, "the ears which God has blessed bow their heads, but these accursed tares stick theirs above the whole field!" For the tare then carries a tall light head of small dark grains which in every respect contrast with the weighty golden ear of the good seed. To try to weed them out is impracticable from the treading down of the wheat and the uprooting of the precious seed-bearers in the attempt. Both must be left together and reaped and threshed together. Then comes the necessary separation. For the ultimate use of the good seed for bread, all the tare grains must be carefully picked out, because they are poisonous. Flour of mixed wheat and tares cannot be given even to animals. Hence all the baskets of wheat are carried from the threshing-floor to the flat roofs of their houses, where they are emptied out on mats, and the tedious separation of grain from grain is carried on, sometimes for days, until the wheat is finally rid of this unhappy admixture. In the rainless summer months of that country the house-tops, which are reached by a flight of steps from the outside, are in constant use for this purpose, as well as for drying their figs, raisins, etc., which fact explains the passage in Matthew xxiv. 17, where he who happens to be on his house-top at the time is enjoined from coming down to take anything from his house. On one occasion, after an early start from a village in Mount Hermon, I felt a dizzy headache coming on which made me uncertain on my horse. My two Arab companions soon complained of the same trouble, till one of them said that he knew by experience what the matter was. "The women of that village where we got our bread this morning were too lazy to get all the *zowan* [tares] out of the wheat. May their days be shortened!" The tare grain, in fact, is in Palestine both a narcotic and an emetic, and much more active in these properties than its congener, the darnel of Europe. It is not a degenerated kind of wheat, as both the natives and many commentators, both ancient and modern, have imagined, but a distinct species, which has no original relationship to wheat or barley.

It is no wonder that the disciples asked to have this parable explained. To their dismay it opened up the prospect of an injury to befall the coming kingdom at its very beginning, and which would last to the end. Men's ideals take no account of imperfections, but here, in equal participation of the field, were to be the good and the radically bad, not in mere propinquity or juxtaposition, but so closely related that no remedy was to be tried. For the command was not to let them *be* together, but a very different matter, to let them *grow* together. We may well ask whether a more inextricable condition of things could be imagined. But however much it perplexed the apostles then, no one now can deny that its representation of our human world is in exact keeping with undeniable fact. Human story is but one long illustration of the strangely intimate relations in this world of its wheat and of its tares. How often do we wonder that so many good men have identified themselves with the worst institutions of history; while, on the other hand, wherever in any age or country a conflict has raged between good and evil, there have been reprobates in plenty among the adherents of the better cause.

More than one purpose of Satan has thus been accomplished. The first is thereby to cast discredit on the whole body of Christ's people. So the saints of the Old Testament are often held up to scorn because they did not grow up in the field of the nineteenth Christian century. But this aspersion ignores altogether the intertwining conditions of life at its very roots, and therefore what it is to grow, as well as to be, in this world.

The second result is to give color to the assertions of a false liberalism. We are told that good men are to be found the world over, whether among Mohammedans, Hindus, Buddhists, or Confucians. The excellent of the earth are not monopolized by one religion.

Hence men can be good without being Christians; why then should Christianity advance such exclusive claims? Then again we are reminded how much true devotion and feeling after God have been discovered the world over by the great modern science of Comparative Religion.

To all such utterances this parable gives a stern and startling answer. The field it speaks of is the world. Not Christian lands, but every land. Not Christian ages or times, but every age and time. Everywhere, therefore, and always, there are and have been good men and bad, but these are so different originally from each other that the end will demonstrate just the reverse of the secret wish of many, that the two kinds, after all, came from the hand of the same Sower. Hence the terms often used in both philosophical and religious discussion about evil this parable stamps as much too abstract and impersonal. Intellectual abstractions are too far away from the heart to awaken either love or fear. Instead of abstractions, instead of sin entering our world as a deadly miasm or gas, or even as a general principle, the parable of the tares pronounces it to be wholly personal in its origin and in all its manifestations. It never exists except as embodied in sinful beings, and therefore the good seed and the tares are the living men and women as contrasted in their native instincts, to whom alone reference is made.

But it is in this world only that the good and the evil can grow together. When the day of the world's harvest shall come, the essential distinction between the two will be made manifest, and a final, because necessary, separation will then take place. Without such separation the whole intent of the sowing of the good seed would be frustrated. This separation, however, cannot be committed either to earthly judgments or to earthly hands. The Son of Man reserves to himself both the time and the agents for its accomplishment.

With our Lord's explicit interpretation that the "field" of this parable is "the world," no exegesis can properly explain the field to be exclusively the Church. Such a misinterpretation, however, has been very common, which maintains that by the tares is prophesied the entrance, with its consequent evils, of worldly men into the fold and enclosure of the Church. Notwithstanding the witness of such lives as that of Socrates the Athenian or Timoleon the Corinthian, this view assumes that the world is Satan's field, with nothing in it but tares, and that Christ came to prepare a new field in Satan's kingdom for good seed only, but in doing so he foresaw that the outside tares were destined to invade it. In that case the terms of the parable should be reversed. The kingdom of heaven should be likened to a man who, in a hidden way, sowed good seed in the field of his enemy, who cultivated only tares, intending thereby that the good seed should ultimately kill out the tares. Now while such a parable would make an awkward figure, its principle is true enough, for it is just the lesson of the parable of the leaven, which foretells the effect on the world of that kingdom which should begin as leaven hid in three measures of meal. But the aspects of truth which these two parables respectively illustrate are very different. That of the leaven contemplates the transforming, yet silent, inner working upon our historical world of the principle of life which Christ brought with him, and which has continued thus to work from the day of the apostles on. The parable of the tares, on the other hand, precedes the parable of the leaven both in time and place. It closes with the Son of Man as Judge at the last day; it begins with his original relation to the human world, when "all things were created through Christ, and unto Christ, and he is before all things, and in him all things hold together" (Col. i. 16, 17). That relation to every human being has never been without its witness, for "he was the true Light, which lighteth every man that cometh into the world" (John i. 9). Therefore, as the beginning of this parable antedates the earthly history of man, so its end is after that history's consummation. Only then will the choice of the elect be justified, when the deep shadows of this world will be dispelled in the light of the kingdom of the Father. But as it is not given to us to know how the Serpent could, and did, enter the garden which the Lord God planted in Eden, neither is it given us here to know how Satan came to enter the field which the Son of Man prepared. The few words, "while men slept," refer to a night utterly impenetrable to our minds now, and whose darkness it is useless for us to attempt to dispel. These words of the second Adam were not intended to clear up the obscurity, in this respect, of the story of the first Adam.

Moreover, as all history down to Christ's day but illustrates the mournful truth of the Fall, so does all history after Christ find its completest epitome in the parable of the tares. Never has there been a fresh beginning for better things in this world without its affording new opportunities of its own making for the growth of tares. Hence have come the sad disappointments of many reformers, who, while rejoicing at the doing away of old evils, as if every evil would then cease, have quite forgotten how men with selfish instincts would find this newly prepared field good for them also. Thus we can imagine how the heroes of liberty in English or American history would be dismayed if they could return now to the scenes of their labors. In view of the rank growth of abuses in our legislative and municipal affairs, how natural it would be for them to exclaim, "Did we not sow good seed in this field? From whence then hath it tares?" Likewise in Church history nothing was more natural than the beginning of monasticism. The world was then everywhere both dangerous and hateful, nor was it as easy then as now to breathe its tainted air and still live a pure Christian life. For a man in those days to retire to the healthy solitude of the desert, in such a climate as that of Egypt, was as much a gain to his soul as it was to his body to leave the pestilential streets of the city. But as time went on, every one of the many attempts to reform monasticism by beginning over again with a new order only repeated the same experience of adding another variety of tares to be called after the pious founder's name.

It is, however, incontestably true that in no other part of the great field of the world would the admixture of the wheat with tares be so exemplified as in the history of the Church. From the first the Church was not allowed to regard a part of the field as hers, about which, therefore, she could erect her own enclosure. Nothing less than the whole field was her right, and hence, in obedience to her native instinct, she went forth to occupy the world. But no sooner did the world perceive that she bid fair to do so, than the world, by its native instinct, proceeded to occupy the Church. It was not alone a corrupt Roman world which was then admitted, but soon afterwards a thoroughly barbarized one, by the so-called conversion of whole races of savages who "embraced" Christianity, often at the summary command of their military leaders. A greater contrast scarcely could be imagined than that between the converts described in the Acts and the converts of that great orthodox champion of the sixth century, the Frankish king Clovis. Nor were he and his fellow-converts different in type from the rest of our European ancestry. Christendom at present comes by lineal descent, not from Peter and Paul, but mainly from Constantine, Charlemagne, Saxon kings, and Norman chieftains. And yet when, or by what earthly wisdom, could this great historical admixture have been prevented? Who was to blame for it?

Soon, however, the baleful influence of the children of the world began to be felt, and in no respect was this more signally developed than in the rise of the doctrine that the Church is a field by itself, with its definite bounds, which as by a pale—ill-omened word!—could both include and exclude. One "pale" after another, therefore, has been erected, without in any case preventing the tares from growing as abundantly as ever within, while much precious seed has remained outside. It has been this old snare of a separate and ideal church without tares which has prompted so many good but grievously mistaken men to disobey the Master's warning not to attempt to pull up the tares on account of the danger to the good seed. Our Lord in Matt. xxv. 37 represents the last day as a day of great surprises in recognition, and surely one of them will be when saintly persecutors and saintly persecuted will then discover how this blinding world prevented them from seeing Christ in each other.

Since the era of the Reformation, however, this disobedience of the Master's injunction about the tares has assumed, with many, a different form, though in practice it is virtually the same as the other, namely, that of transplanting the good seed into a more or less small enclosure of their own preparing. Judging also from the little but rigid bounds which some have thus chosen, it would appear as if they would fain pot the heavenly seed! But as botanists assure us that the North American continent now abounds with European weeds which colonists unwittingly introduced with the grains which they brought with them, so the universality of the law of the spiritual tares has never escaped illustration in the history of our religious sects, from the largest to the smallest of them.

As naturally might be expected, this profound parable has excited much controversy. Archbishop Trench remarks that over the words " the field is the world " a " great battle has been fought, greater, perhaps, than over any single phrase in Scripture, if we except the consecrating words of the holy eucharist." From the disputes of Augustine with the Donatists down to our own day this text has been appealed to against separatists from the body of the Church, as condemning all who leave her communion because it contains either ungodly men or those who teach errors of doctrine. So this text does, as far as its words go; but it is curious to note how the risk of depending on mere texts is illustrated here by the fact that they who use it for this purpose invariably garble the text itself in order to have it support their contention. They always quote the text as if the term "world" in it means, not the world, but the Church. Now if our Lord had said, the field is the kingdom of God on earth, then not only the Donatists, but the major part of Christendom, would be in much perplexity whether they are now in the kingdom or not. Who is to decide between the ancient orthodox Eastern Church, the Roman Catholic, the Anglican, and the other Protestant communions as to which holds the "field"? The decision cannot be by a comparison as to which "pale" has the most tares, for each has its share of them, but which has the most to show of good seed. This test seems to be the last one thought of by these controversialists, who, instead, appeal rather to the antiquity of date in the erection of their respective enclosures.

Other discussions have arisen whether by the good seed and the tares we are to infer that there is such a generic difference between men originally that neither kind could ever become the other. Our Lord himself has illustrated his doctrine about the relationship of Satan to men in this world, as far as he saw fit for us to go. To men who boasted of their descent from Abraham (which he did not dispute), but who were then planning to murder him, he said: "Ye are of your father the devil, and the lusts of your father it is your will to do. He was a murderer from the beginning" (John viii. 44). In contrast with men of such instincts we read that to those who receive Christ "gave he the right to them to become children of God, to be born not of blood [descent], nor of the will of the flesh, nor of the will of man, but of God" (John i. 12, 13). In each case a close relationship through a deep communion of spirit is asserted, which truth is all that concerns us now to know.

We may remark here that many of the divergencies in exposition of the parables have arisen from attempts to use them in polemics, as if doctrinal formularies could be derived from them. Isolated texts from the parables thus were made often to do duty in the construction of Church dogmas, or for deciding Church controversies, with the result, of course, that every part, or even word, in the parable had to have its definite setting, as plainly indicated as if it were a stone in a perfect arch. But the fact should be emphasized that the parables, from their very nature, were intended, not to *define* truth, but to *illustrate* it, and an illustration never can be made synonymous with a proposition. Indeed, one might as well try to represent an apple-tree in beauteous blossom by drawing a diagram of it, as to show how one or other phrase in a parable corresponds to the articles of a creed.

The parables are stories of life from full daylight, not theses from lamplit desks. In a contract it is needful that the precise meaning of each important word should be settled carefully, and creeds often, very properly, do duty as contracts when any one solemnly accepts them in public, or subscribes to them on assuming the duties of an office. In this world of deceptions creeds are as necessary as any other binding engagements, and in the Gospels and Epistles there are all the requisite elements for making them, but not in the parables. As illustrations of God's truth the parables are invaluable, because they are so replete with life that their suggestiveness often is both more and deeper than we can safely attempt to formulate in set theological terms. Thus the part which Satan takes in this parable strongly suggests that man's story, as we know it, is not a beginning, but a link in the story of the intelligent universe. But no statement of the kind would be in place in any Christian creed.

We do not imply by these remarks a disparagement of creeds. On the contrary, a creed holds the same relation to a religion that obtains between the human body and its bony framework. On the perfection of the skeleton depends the effectiveness of the whole voluntary motor system of muscles, whilst the most living element of the blood, the red cells, owe their origin and constant renewal to the marrow of the bones. It is only with the simplest organisms that no skeleton is needed, because they can move, secrete, and digest equally well in every part. So he who can adapt himself to all doctrines, and share his sympathies impartially between Christians, spiritualists, agnostics, or atheists, is but an intellectual polyp, who suffers no more inconvenience from dividing sentiments in his soul than a polyp does when his body is cut up. Instead of dividing the Church, its future reunion is to come by creed, when the whole Church adequately appreciates the great fact that on the doctrines about the person of Christ there is even now but one Christian creed.

In conclusion, we may say that, as with all our Lord's parables, the parable of the tares contains its own special and great practical lesson, but meant in this case for Christians rather than for men of the world. A Divine patience, so to speak, is enjoined upon men on account of their fellow-men. The good and the evil are not found here as genuine and counterfeit coins may be heaped together. If that were so the services to the Church of heresy experts or specialists in orthodoxy would be of great value. But the good seed and the tares are contemplated as growing together, not only in community of blood or race, but even, it may be, in the same family household. No more touching scene of love and affection can be found described than that of the parting of Paul with his weeping friends of Ephesus (Acts xx.). Yet even then the teaching of this parable came to his mind, as he said, "I know that from among your own selves shall men arise, speaking perverse things to draw away the disciples after them." If with such a teacher as Paul, and in those days when there was comparatively so little temptation for worldly men to enter the Church, nevertheless the tares were already taking root along with the good seed, how can we expect to be free from perverse men in the Church now? That they should be rebuked and warned against is as much a Christian duty now as ever, but both this parable and the verdict of history is against the dividing of the Church on their account. The evangelical branches of the Church especially have had more than enough of these ruinous uprootings in the past. Wiser would it be to accept the simple thought of the Syrian peasants, who to this day believe that tares can best be kept down by nourishing to the utmost the life of the good seed.

THE DRAW-NET

Matt. xiii., 47-50.

Again, the kingdom of heaven is like unto a net, that was cast into the sea, and gathered of every kind: Which, when it was full, they drew to shore, and sat down, and gathered the good into vessels, but cast the bad away. So shall it be at the end of the world; the angels shall come forth, and sever the wicked from among the just, And shall cast them into the furnace of fire: there shall be wailing and gnashing of teeth.

THE DRAW-NET

Saida, the present successor of the ancient city of Sidon, the Zidon of the times of Jacob (Gen. xlix. 13), is beautifully situated on a point which, jutting out from the general trend of the sea-shore, forms on the north a gently curved beach some three miles in length and about two hundred yards in width, where it meets the hedge line of the orange gardens for which the town is famous. During five pleasantly spent years in that city I would often time my evening walk so as to watch the fishermen draw their nets, about sundown, upon that stretch of soft sand. Before my first experience of the kind, I was not at all prepared for the large scale on which this work is done, nor for the immense size of the nets. At early dawn a fleet of boats may be seen close to a long line of huge floating corks, extending far out upon the glassy surface of the sea. The vast net, in fact, is dropped down ere the stars fade, and as the day wears on one end is brought to land by some of the boats, while the other is slowly swung round in a great sweep by the united tow of the others, and not till the close of a hard day's toil do the two ends approach each other, and the fishermen turn to and pull it up on shore. Then comes the exciting time for seeing whether the catch will repay the heavy labor of the day. On one occasion I heard a more than usual outbreak of fishermen's imprecations. For variety of terms Arab cursing cannot be surpassed, though in all countries fishermen are unfortunately noted for bad language, as our own English "billingsgate" testifies. The reason for this particular chorus of oaths I soon saw in a strange, dark-looking mass, evidently of fishes, rolling over and over in the net meshes as it was yet heaving in the breaking waves. It proved to be a large shoal of sting-rays, a fish which is a flat, leathery, ungainly-looking creature, resembling our flounder, but armed with a long tapering tail ending in a sharp barbed spine, which is a dangerous weapon both for offence and defence.* When these are numerous, other fishes are apt to be scarce in the catch, and so the baskets were but half filled, while the discarded rays were left upon the sand. At times the dreaded electrical torpedo is landed, while at others the Sidon fishermen are driven to distraction by immense shoals of sardines, for, as the Arabs do not know how to preserve them, they simply leave them to poison the air with their decaying heaps. At no time is their catch good throughout, for the Mediterranean teems with a wonderful variety of life, including "each kind of badness," as every fisherman there will feelingly tell you.

I may remark in passing that these Moslem fishermen interested me for reasons which they would not have suspected. One elder among them, who faithfully fulfilled his promise to bring a torpedo fish alive, was a devout,

---

* The case of a New Jersey fisherman attracted a good deal of notice in our New York newspapers a few years ago, who was killed by one of these fishes which he drew into his boat, and which severed an artery in his leg by a single blow of its tail, so that he bled to death before assistance could reach him from other boats.

simple-hearted man, who refused pay out of gratitude for a small medical favor. It was easy to recognize a good groundwork in his nature. But, as a class, the fishermen of Saida would not be very different from the ancient fishermen of Galilee. So little has been the change that dress, habits, manners, and even turns of colloquial expression still remain to afford living, yet perfectly corresponding, object-lessons of the origin of our apostles. Especially is the mental correspondence complete, whether we regard the stock of general ideas possible to either as a class, or the religious conceptions that would occur to men living under the traditional rule of Jewish Pharisees or of Mohammedan ulems. If so, then, humanly speaking, no "fishers of men," or persons capable of drawing into captivity multitudes of other men, could be obtained from either company. The "environment" about which some philosophic writers have so much to say, renders this simply inconceivable. The chair of St. Peter, or the court of St. James, indeed! How could the names of those Syrian fishermen have become so strangely associated? Not to speak of Oriental fishermen, where among fishermen the world over could the makers of great history be found?

On natural principles it is as inevitable that a man's mental horizon should be bounded by the conditions of his life, as that his physical horizon should depend upon the place where he stands. The Moslem fishermen of our day live in a world of thought which is wholly dominated by the great literary caste of the ulema, or students of the Koran. Starting with the postulate that every letter, vowel, and dot of that book was brought down from God by the archangel Gabriel, it follows that nothing can equal in worth and importance the learning of God's own language, and hence the life of the ulem is spent in the heavy study of the laws of Arabic grammar. The Arabs, therefore, boast that they have twenty-five thousand books on this sacred science in their literature. The world has scarcely seen such an example of the concentration of human toil on mere words, or such a wilderness of laborious pedants as Islam presents. We have to go back to the doctors of the law in Christ's day to find a parallel to it.

The reward is a superstitious veneration on the part of the common people for the learned sheikh, which is wafted as a sweet-smelling savor to his nostrils whenever he appears in the market-place. But nothing possibly can so stir the human heart to anger as to suggest to such a man that all this deference of his fellows is misplaced because there is a better wisdom than his, and that all his life's labor has been misdirected and will come to naught! Hence, towards a representative of a Christian civilization, the glance of hate in a ulem's eye is simply indicative of that spirit which prompts those recurrent terrible massacres of Oriental Christians by Mohammedans, of which the world has by no means witnessed the last. It is begotten of the same origin as that literary caste malignity which pursued our Saviour until it exulted in his crucifixion. This very expression, *aami*, "this multitude," "which knoweth not the law, are accursed" (John vii. 49), I have myself repeatedly heard from the lips of Arab literati as they referred to the common herd, and, of course, it would be peculiarly applicable to such as fishermen. The fishermen, on the other hand, humbly receive this estimate as no more than their due. To regard themselves as near the holy level of the doctors of their law and classical language would never enter their minds. In everything, and especially in speech, they feel themselves to be altogether vile. It was thoroughly natural, therefore, in Peter, though in him there spoke also a genuine feeling, for him to "fall down at Jesus' knees, saying, "Depart from me, for I am a sinful man, O Lord" (Luke v. 8). But what a solemn lesson, nevertheless, did that dear good soul give of the lasting heart-pang which an old, long-forsaken evil habit may yet occasion by its sudden revival when least expected! "But he began to curse and to swear, I know not this man of whom ye speak!"

The parable of the draw-net, therefore, the apostles could well understand. Unlike the parable of the tares, which was given to the whole multitude, our Lord gave this to them as they gathered around him in private.

The difference in scope between the two parables explains this. That of the tares applied to the whole world of mankind from its beginning. This applies rather to the history of the Church in that world. Therefore, in this parable the world is the sea, in which live fish of every kind, and the Church is to be a great net let down to gather men out of that sea. No comparison thus could have made plainer to the minds of those fishermen that the Church was destined in the future to extend immensely, for the net is much larger than the field of any sower. But clearly enough it taught them also that the fishing for men by them, and by their successors, was to bring within the great folds of the Church many other than saints, even the worst kinds of the creatures with which they were too familiar. It was not enough that they should think of the kingdom as sharing the common lot of the world itself in being a tare-strewn field; for even when the Church should have its definite bounds, like a strong net in the sea, it would still draw within itself the bad with the good. There is no way for opening a net, while it is being drawn, to let out the bad only. The separation must be left to the last, when the object of the whole labor will be found in the good kinds alone which have been secured.

This parable, indeed, emphasizes the lesson which the apostles, like all true Christians also, would be slow to learn, and therefore would need to have reiterated to them. The Church of Christ is a sacred and a beautiful ideal. No words of the New Testament are so strong or so tender as those which describe the sweet, blessed bride of the Lord. Why cannot we always think of her without a single association of evil? Let the world be a field where Satan walked by night; but since Jesus came to bring his own, why should he not draw them out of the world to himself, to be a peculiar people, a holy nation, and all within the same great fold? But Jesus in the parables is a prophet, not an idealist, and the prophets of the Lord were not wont to speak, as human imagination ever prompts, of a coming earthly perfection. History exactly fulfilled his words. His Church has become a thing of vast extent in the world; but let no one think that because he is within the Church therefore must he be gathered with the chosen of God at the last.

THE MUSTARD-SEED

Matt. xiii., 31–32.

Another parable put he forth unto them, saying, The kingdom of heaven is like to a grain of mustard seed, which a man took, and sowed in his field: Which indeed is the least of all seeds: (Mark. is less than all the seeds that be in the earth) but when it is grown, it is the greatest among herbs, and becometh a tree, so that the birds of the air come and lodge in the branches thereof.

THE MUSTARD-SEED

The four parables of the sower, the seed growing secretly, the tares, and the draw-net certainly had much in them to disappoint both the multitude and the disciples. Instead of their cherished visions of a mighty kingdom suddenly appearing and accomplishing the conquest of the world in their generation, these parables intimated at best a very gradual development, accompanied by much seeming failure. The King was to be like a sower who failed three times out of four to get any return for his labor, and what success he had was not at all uniform in degree. Then, in complete contrast with the dazzling apparition of Alexander's kingdom, the kingdom of the Son of David was to increase as silently and imperceptibly as a seed unfolds itself—too slowly for any bystander to watch it grow. Again, he was to be like a man whose whole work was irretrievably damaged by the malice of an enemy; and, finally, ere his kingdom of heaven became in fact what it had been in name, many of his followers would be found so wholly unfit for it that they would be cast away.

In the four parables, however, of the mustard-seed, the leaven, the hid treasure, and the pearl the prophecy is one of unqualified success. The first pair, the mustard-seed and the leaven, illustrate the two great aspects of the kingdom in its relation to the world. That of the mustard-seed foretells how, as regards its external manifestation, beginning with a gathering of 120 souls in an upper chamber in Jerusalem, a Christendom was to grow which would attract to itself many diverse races of men; while that of the leaven tells of that within it which no birds of the air can see nor any animals know, for Influence belongs only to the high realm of spiritual beings, and therefore is outwardly known only by its effects.

The second pair, the hid treasure and the pearl, go straight to the heart. In them the kingdom is no general cause of country, race, or church, but a fact of overpowering individual love. Men and women are represented with their own personal discoveries of a preciousness in it which none but heirs of heaven could make, for at once every earthly possession is surrendered by them for the exchange. Their discovery is the King himself! For the joy of meeting him at his appearing many thousands in all ages have willingly laid down their lives. In no respect does history ever fail abundantly to fulfil the prophecies of the parables.

The characterization of the mustard-seed as "less than all the seeds that be in the earth" (Mark iv. 31) was as truthful a statement by our Lord as when, in the parable of the sower, he said, "when the sun was risen" (R. V.), though in neither case was he scientifically accurate, for the sun never rises, and botanists know of smaller seeds than those of mustard. But truthfulness and accuracy are not necessarily synonymous terms. Nothing can be more accurate than a photograph from life, for no inaccuracy can be detected in it even by a microscope. But people will continue to prefer and to pay for an expensive portrait by a skilled artist, with all his human mistakes, rather than for the sorry likenesses which the accurate sun often makes of their friends. Our Lord was speaking to the people of seeds which they daily used, and whose strong growth was before their eyes, for the purpose of emphasizing the apparent insignificance in its beginning which would characterize the kingdom of heaven. The illustration of the parable lies in the smallness of the mustard-seed compared with other seeds, rather than in the greatness of the subsequent development, for if the latter were his object, the familiar instance of the acorn and the oak would have answered better. Yet even in this respect the soil of Gennesaret furnishes an example striking enough in the size of its mustard-plants, especially just about the shores of the lake.

All around the Lake of Tiberias, on its eastern as well as along its western borders, numerous hot springs pour forth their waters, making the shores in many places yellow with their deposits of sulphur. These, when dry, are raised by the winds, to descend upon the surrounding soil, rendering it, therefore, peculiarly adapted to cause the mustard-plant to flourish beyond what it does probably anywhere else in the world. The mustard-seed, as is well known, is remarkable for the large proportion of sulphur which it contains, and which exists in it in a peculiar chemical combination or principle to which the activity of mustard is due. This activity, however, does not pre-exist in the seed, for it is not called forth until the seed has been crushed and mixed with water. Birds, therefore, can eat the seed with impunity, and in the proper season the traveller on Gennesaret may ride by mustard-bushes as high as his horse, and alive with flocks of merry bullfinches or of rock-pigeons feeding upon the seeds.

As just remarked, the particular lesson of this parable is not the wonderful increase, simply as such, of Christ's kingdom in the world from a small beginning, though this is now the most salient fact of history. Other great religions have grown also from a small following at first of their single founders. The personal ministry of Mohammed was more than twice as long as that of Jesus ere he could count seventy disciples. It is, therefore, not by numerical estimate, but rather when we compare the seed-principle of each of these historical religions, that the true wonder of Christ's kingdom is revealed. We cannot, indeed, illustrate better what a little mustard-seed in the field of human nature the Gospel seems at its beginning, when measured with the moral obstacles which it had to overcome, than to cite the contrasts between Christianity and Islam, which even their many historic parallels only serve to intensify. Thus, both these religions are of Shemitic origin, and both have led great races, wholly foreign to the Shemitic world, to exchange their native religions for an earnest devotion to the one personal God of Shem. As the apostles went forth from Judea after the death of their Master to found a Christendom, so it was after the death of Mohammed that the remarkable body of men, "the Companions of the Prophet," issued forth from Arabia to found the wide realm of Islam. But long ere this the parallelism gives place to contrasts. Instead of the scene on Palm-Sunday, when

Jesus came, a few days before his death, to the city which rejected him, Mohammed returned, a short time before his death, to the Mecca which had spurned him, at the head of 114,000 of the best warriors and robbers of the world. But does history find it difficult to explain that Arab gathering to the standard of such a successful marauder as Mohammed had by that time proved himself to be? He was only different from the savage Soudan Mahdi of this age in being the first of the kind. From the day that a race, predatory by custom and by descent, was summoned by Mohammed to a war upon all mankind, every distinctive feature of Islam, whether in its past or its present, is found to be based upon easily understood motives of human nature. Thus nothing could be more welcome to the heart of the natural man than Mohammed's compromise, by a mere easily repeated sentence, between Allah and the old human passions for combat and for bodily license. Taught that they can be Allah's sole elect, not only without any inner cross to bear, but enjoined to call and to treat all other people as dogs, Moslems can be extremely devout in speech while ever ready to wage religious war by tongue and by sword on all the world. As man's oldest and most natural enemy is man, so the follower of this Ishmaelitish religion finds it in constant harmony with his native instincts. What, therefore, the life of the original seed in these two religions was is shown by the first definite step of each in its development. Christianity as an aggressive movement began with the Day of Pentecost — that day which wholly transformed the apostles from the men which they had been, in thought, word, and act, into the men who established the Church in the world. Islam, likewise, by a true instinct, dates its beginning, not from Mohammed's first preaching in his native city, but from his Hegira, or flight from Mecca, for that event wholly transformed him from a preacher against the old Arab religions into a man of the sword, and a man who, for planning and for executing cold-blooded assassinations of individuals or massacres of whole bodies of men, has few superiors

in history except among his own followers.
Hence it was but a natural outcome of the
spirit of the Hegira that Mohammed's own
apostles soon fell to murdering each other,
and that his trusted body-guard, the Ansar,
were all shockingly butchered, with their
wives and children, leaving such memories
that the graves of the first three caliphs, who
correspond as pillars in the church of Islam
to Peter, James, and John in the Church of
Christ, have still to be guarded night and day
from insults by the followers of Ali, whom
these caliphs treacherously supplanted. As
it began from the Hegira with a marauder,
Islam has continued ever since so to foster
the marauding spirit that in no generation of
its twelve centuries have men been able to
travel unarmed from one city to another in
any country where it has borne sway. The
constant danger which any peaceable traveller encounters now in Morocco, in Arabia
itself, or in Afghanistan, is but a repetition
of the same old story, for never in the high
days of the caliphs of Bagdad or in Spain
could caravans be dispensed with. The best

development to which Arab rule ever attained would fairly correspond with the Italy of the Borgias. Mohammedan pilgrims have always had to fight or to buy their way, as they do still, to reach Mecca itself. Moslems, indeed, cease to rob and to kill each other, as well as other people, only where Christian power compels them to keep the peace.

That religion should ally herself with human passions and inclinations was no new thing in the world, as the religions of antiquity everywhere prove. But what was reserved to Islam was to make the God of the Old and of the New Testament likewise acceptable to the original bent of human nature, and especially to man's dominant passion, pride. But did Christianity offer any such allurement when her voice was first heard? Rather, we cannot emphasize the difference in this respect too strongly, for if there be one term fitly descriptive of her most characteristic aspect to the world it would be—the Religion of Humiliation. Whence, therefore, the attraction, or what the promise of success in a cause which must always maintain the attitude of confession? Even now, and in Christian lands, many find it is not easy to confess Christ. That fact of itself implies an element in Christianity which never fails to run counter to the most constant of human inclinations, the passion for superiority. But if it be so now, what must it have been in the beginning, when this seed was the least of all the seeds that were in the earth? A despised Galilean village gave her Founder its name, and which is still perpetuated with characteristic scorn by Islam as the one designation for all Christians—the Nazarenes. How natural, also, were the feelings of contempt and of hate aroused in most Jews at the occasion of Pilate's insult, not so much to Jesus as to them, in his trilingual inscription, "This is the King of the Jews"—fitly on a cross! Love and scorn are much wider apart than love and enmity, and thus all the facts show that more than mere hostility had to be overcome ere a Jew, with his native conception of his expected Messiah, could be brought to accept the man of Nazareth as his king. As a whole the nation chose to die first.

7

But when we turn from the Jews to the rest of the contemporary world, how could the prospect for growth of the new seed there be more unlikely? The Jews themselves were throughout the Roman world already a proverb of dislike, or as Tacitus tersely designates them, a repulsive people. Their expectation of a Jewish conqueror of the world was as well known as it was despised, so that the very title of Messiah was a term for ridicule. When Paul, therefore, said that he had nothing to tell about save a Messiah, and him crucified, we generally fail to appreciate the wonder of this message to the men who first heard it, on account of our very different and sacred associations with the word cross. To their ears it came, a Jewish Messiah, and a gibbeted Messiah at that! That in a contest then to the death, continuing through three centuries between the wonderfully organized power of Rome and the wholly unarmed Church, it was the Church which conquered, has been the problem of history for explanation, because the struggle lasted too long for the result to be ascribed either to fortune or to individuals.

But a more impressive testimony still to her inherent vitality was the spread of Christianity among the savage races who overthrew Rome, because historically it began while they were yet beyond the Rhine, and in the first instance is traced to captives whom they had taken in their incursions into Roman territory. It has been well said that by the time the Northern invaders finally subdued the empire they had become already better Christians than the Romans were. That ere that period the mustard-seed had become a tree, with the birds flocking to its branches, was strikingly shown when Rome herself was saved by appealing to the German tribes, who had stripped her of everything except Italy, to make head with her against the terrible pagan Hun, and to overthrow Attila on the field of Chalons, because he came to destroy the Church of Christ. The question naturally arises, How came those shaggy warriors to be imbued with a reverence for that Name? What could be further from the ideal of fierce manliness of the old Teutonic hero than this image of meek saintliness? Yet so it was then, and ever has been since, that a mighty Christendom has grown apace in the world, more and more uniting the nations by bonds of principle and of sentiment which mark them off very distinctly from the peoples of either Islam, Brahminism, or Buddhism. Whatever be the thoughts of men about Jesus, none can deny that his forecast in this parable has been quite fulfilled, in that his kingdom in its external development has become the greatest growth of history.

THE LEAVEN

Matt. xiii., 33.

Another parable spake he unto them; The kingdom of heaven is like unto leaven, which a woman took, and hid in three measures of meal, till the whole was leavened.

THE LEAVEN

Notwithstanding the uncertainty which prevails as to the exact equivalents in modern terms of ancient measures, it cannot be doubted that the three measures of meal which constituted the Hebrew ephah of this parable amounted to more than an English bushel in quantity. To us this would appear as more than what a large family would use at one baking, but the conditions of ordinary Palestinian life do not render it at all unusual. Accustomed as we are to a great variety of food, including an abundance of meat, we use bread more as an accompaniment to, than as the chief article of, a meal. But in our Saviour's time, as well as now, the main food of the people was fermented milk, cheese, olives and oil, figs, raisins, and bread. It will be seen by this that bread is literally the staff of life with them, to which all else is subsidiary, and therefore that the statement of the parable simply conforms to the familiar facts of household economy in that land. This fact, however, it served to illustrate, that it would not be a small world which finally would become wholly leavened by the kingdom of heaven!

As in the case of the term "seed," so we may say that to this parable of the leaven modern science gives a peculiar significance which was wholly unknown in the times when the parable was first uttered. Then, and until very lately, it was supposed that the leavening of bread was caused by an inanimate material acting by purely physical processes upon the meal which it fermented. This was the view which the distinguished chemist Liebig maintained to the last, but the illustrious Pasteur has effected the greatest and most important revolution in history, so far as the physical life of mankind is concerned, by his epoch-making researches on what fermentation really is. It was by these researches that the vitally important relations became known of the microscopic forms of life to the visible animal and vegetable kingdoms, whether in the processes of health or those of disease and death. Pasteur has demonstrated, to the acceptance of the whole scientific world, that ferments are not portions of lifeless organic matter which set up their changes by their mere presence in fermentable substances, but are instead actually living organisms, and that the fermentation which they occasion is a necessary consequence or manifestation of their vital activity and growth. As he expresses it, "the conversion can only take place when the material to be fermented comes into actual contact with the living protoplasm of the ferment." One result, however, of the action of these living cells is the formation of what may be termed pervasive chemical principles, which extend to some distance from the cells into the surrounding fermentable material, profoundly, though at first scarcely visibly, modifying it, and preparing it for the subsequent extension to it of the growing ferment.

Another development from these discoveries is that the variety of organisms which are capable of inducing fermentation is seemingly limitless. This in fact constitutes one of the greatest practical difficulties in producing many of the fermentations in common use, for the desired result is often utterly vitiated by the contamination of the proper ferment by the entrance with it of some form of what is technically termed a " wild " yeast, which may grow so as wholly to supplant with its evil working the action of a " cultivated " yeast. How to procure a "pure" yeast is therefore one of the most carefully investigated problems of this branch of economic chemistry.

With these preliminaries, we can now turn to the great lessons of this parable about the Kingdom of God. The leavening of the world of which it speaks refers to much deeper and more hidden results than those aspects of the kingdom to which the parable of the mustard-seed corresponds. Even the most superficial observer cannot overlook the Church in the world, while the true effect of her being there might be entirely unperceived by him. The surface of the meal before the whole is leavened often appears much the same that it ever was, notwithstanding the great change which has already occurred within.

There is, in fact, nothing more hidden than the springs of human conduct. Often they are deeper than the consciousness of their possessors, and this parable refers just to that element in human life which reaches down below beliefs and opinions, customs and laws, to the sources of them all in the motives and promptings of the spirit. In more senses than one it is the spirit which is the life, for thence proceed both belief and conduct. Therefore we can speak just as properly of the spirit of an age as we can of the spirit of an individual. We recognize by such a phrase not so much the prevailing sentiments or opinions of an age as that profounder animating element which makes opinions and sentiments prevail.

Thus we are often told in these days that it is useless to enact good laws unless there exist a public sentiment which will enforce them. But what is this public sentiment without which law might as well not be? It assumes no outward form, often indeed, it is not even articulate. It owes its existence instead to the intercommunion of human minds and spirits. Our very word "community," when applied to people residing together, is a recognition of the great fact that men cannot be together without becoming sharers in each others' lives. From one to the other, from the highest to the humblest and back again, there are constantly passing streams of influence, acting and reacting until not a life escapes being very different on that account from what it would have been by itself, or from what it would have been in a very different "community." A public sentiment, therefore, is born of the passing of thought and of feeling, often unconsciously, from one living soul to another, just as the vital working of the leavening cells passed silently from particle to particle in the three measures of meal.

That a great change has come over the spirit of men just where the branches of the tree of the first parable overshadow them, but nowhere beyond, is evident enough, though how that change has come about is disputed. Many strive to regard it as spontaneous, or maintain, as Matthew Arnold expresses it, that there is a stream or tendency which makes for righteousness, whose origin is as unknown as the force of gravitation. That this stream or tendency is found only in Christendom is looked upon by such minds as but a coincidence. But the facts are these: One who lived when the leaven was first hid in the meal only confirmed the accounts by Roman writers themselves of the spirit of the age when he described the men of that world as "filled with all unrighteousness, wickedness, covetousness, maliciousness; full of envy, murder, strife, deceit, malignity; whisperers, backbiters, haters of God, insolent, haughty, boasters, inventors of evil things, disobedient to parents, without understanding, covenant-breakers, without natural affection, unmerciful"! (Rom. i. 29-31). Not a word of this terrible indictment can be denied, for Roman poets, philosophers, and historians only amplify it as they describe their contemporaries. A people whose continuous amusement was to see gladiators slaughtered, or aged slaves crucified, simply enjoyed cruelty. We naturally shrink from the thought that this race had much in common with us, and would fain hope that such a species of mankind has forever passed away. But from my own personal knowledge I am sure that whole communities of Mohammedans now would enjoy just such spectacles of the slaughter of Christians which the proletariat of Rome did under Nero. At present, in British India, the moral chasm which separates the European from the Asiatic in their respective sentiments about truth and human brotherhood is so great that neither side understands the other at all. It is no insult to an Asiatic to be called a liar, and cruelty he regards as akin to courage. When the volcanic explosion occurs there, which may happen at any time, the utter powerlessness of such agencies as a free press, railroads, telegraphs, and the rest of alleged world transformers to leaven human nature with true goodness will be startlingly proven. That this is not because it is Asiatic, but because it is human nature which is in question, is shown by the fact that where, even in Europe, men are found who in common reject Christianity and her God, the same unleavened spirit manifests itself on occasion as of old. The strongest light of modern civilization in France certainly showed no sweetness of effect on the Communards of 1870. These truths amply prove that the meal in the measure neither can nor has changed itself, but that it is changed only by a new life put into it, which works according to its own laws into effects caused alone by its presence and growth. But as leavening comes only by a living process, so Christians should never forget that only by the pervading effects of a true Christian life can the world be leavened!

And what wondrous transformations has it produced, though scarcely as yet has it fully permeated even one of the three measures! Little by little, its hidden influence on the hearts of individuals generated a new spirit in the world of virtue and kindliness, which purified the home, made men sick of the sight of blood in the amphitheatre, lessened progressively the awful evils of ancient slavery till it ended slavery itself, visited the sick and sought out the prisoner, until finally its spirit has spread to the field of battle itself, and enjoined the same tender and skilled care for a wounded enemy as for a wounded comrade. In the world of Islam men cannot trust one another enough even to form a commercial company, so that the marvels produced by such co-operation in our trading or industrial fields are a mystery to them. This is only one of many illustrations of that blessed unifying life which has entered our poor warring world, everywhere permeating the springs of human nature with that new sense of mutual obligation which can be satisfied with nothing short of truth, justice, mercy, and good-will towards all. Was not the coming of that kingdom, whose beneficent influence would thus extend alike to all the concerns of human life, justly named Glad Tidings to all the world?

It was to meet the narrowness of human view that the parable of the leaven forms so needful an accompaniment to the parable of the mustard-seed. Our Lord's kingdom in the world is a subject too great and too many-sided to have even one of its aspects adequately represented by a single illustration. An undue attention to the important truth which the parable of the mustard-seed enforces has led, in fact, to two widely prevalent, though opposite, forms of error. The growth of the mustard-seed corresponds, as we have seen, to the visible growth in the world of the Church. So great and imposing has that been that multitudes accordingly have been more attracted by this aspect of the kingdom than by any other. There have been, therefore, many who were more zealous as churchmen than as Christians. Moreover, as only one mustard-seed is spoken of as planted, so it has been argued that there could be only one visible Church, and hence external evidences of her place and relative growth have been much relied upon to support the claims of contending parties. But in the kingdom as a hidden leaven in the world there is a lesson which opposes this whole tendency, for the criterion which it establishes is not how much of the world has been overshadowed by the Church, or by her branches, but how much has the world by her been changed in spirit, and brought nearer to the fulfilment of the prayer that the will of God become also the will of man on earth.

The external view of the Church, on the other hand, has led many to charge Christianity with a host of wrongs and shortcomings which historically have been associated with her name. Thus the Roman world became nominally Christian, and likewise in turn the European nations which succeeded Rome. But naming a thing is not changing it, and hence Christianity through the centuries has had to bear the reproach of numberless manifestations of the old unleavened world of human evil working under the cover of her sacred name. It is a cause for thankfulness, therefore, that as time goes on the unnatural alliance of the Church and the world is lapsing by Providential limitation. The murderers of the French Commune and the anarchists of our day are the descendants, both natural and spiritual, of the murderers of St. Bartholomew's Day, but they no longer call themselves Christians or children of the true Church. With each generation the essential antagonism of the spirit of Christ's kingdom, and the spirit of the world is becoming more and more recognized, thus imparting a greater unity to both sides. But while this may result in apparently a sharper conflict than ever for the Church, yet to those who look beneath the surface every indication of our times is that the leaven of the kingdom is permeating the world more rapidly than in any preceding age, according to the law of life that the more the individual cells multiply the more others like them are born. Rather it is significant of the spread of the true leaven that unbelief itself is now obliged to borrow the garb of Christian ethics, and to preach the gospel of Altruism as the hope of humanity.

The disturbing element in certain sought-for fermentations through the contamination with "wild" yeasts, which we have mentioned above as revealed by modern investigations, is not without its striking spiritual parallels in the history of the Church. Nothing so impresses the reader of Church history as the amazing multiplication of Gnostic and other heretical sects in the first centuries of the Church's career. Scarcely had she been freed from her conflict with the Judaizing teachers of the apostolic times than the Greek world supplied a crowd of invaders who threatened completely to overrun her field with their noxious speculative growths. That they and so many other forms of evil doctrine have all in turn become extinct, is a greater testimony to the possession of a divinely imparted life in the Church than her survival from the conflicts with her external foes in the world.

THE HID TREASURE

Matt. xiii., 44.

Again, the kingdom of heaven is like unto treasure hid in a field; the which when a man hath found, he hideth, and for joy thereof goeth and selleth all that he hath, and buyeth that field.

THE HID TREASURE

What it is to find a hid treasure in Syria was once well illustrated during my residence in Sidon. A land-owner of the town had hired a band of seventeen peasants, men and women, to dig up a field of about an acre to plant it with orange-trees. For such a purpose the custom is to run close together parallel trenches about three feet in depth, and then turn the soil into them until the whole field is thus gone over. As I watched them from the windows of our house on the city wall, I was amused at the slowness of their work, one man pushing into the soft sandy soil a long wooden shovel, which was then pulled out by another with a rope. For such labor the daily wages of the men was about twelve cents of our money, and of the women nine, paid in the wretched, dark-looking Turkish piastre, which is a thin piece of copper with a trace of a silver coating. One day two of the men while in a trench turned up a leaden box more than a foot long, and as the man with the spade was a dull fellow his companion lifted it out and threw it under a fig-tree near by, remarking, "This is nothing but an old relic; we will see what it contains by-and-by." In a moment, however, another box was also unearthed, which, on being struck with the spade, let out a stream of glittering pieces of gold! In a moment the whole seventeen men and women were upon the spot in a heap, fighting and screaming as only Arabs can at such a sight, until one of them sagely called for silence lest their hubbub would attract others to share the prize with them. "Let us quietly dig," said he, "and see if there be any more of these precious boxes, and then at night we will divide the treasure equally between us." His advice was followed, when a third box was found, and, as the sequel showed, very probably a fourth. Unfortunately, at their nocturnal division, one of the women thought that she did not receive her full share, and in revenge she stole away to the *mutsellim*, or Moslem governor's house, and, showing him some of the pieces, that official lost no time to collect his guard, and to sally out and capture the whole company before they had separated. The next day the entire city was in a ferment at the news, and soon the British consular agent at Sidon called at our house with an account of his interference with the governor to stop his torturing the unfortunate peasants so as to wring from them the full secret of the find. This the consul had a right to do, as the Turkish government had stipulated with the European powers to abolish torture in the Sultan's dominions. The scene which he described was graphic enough: of the *mutsellim*, with a wide silk *keffeeyeh* spread on the rug before him, with a larger pile of gold coins thereon than any Sidonian had ever beheld, while the poor creatures were screaming under an ancient form of thumb-torture inflicted upon them by the savage Moslem guard. By the representation of the European consular agents the poor fellows were at last released, and even some of the money obtained from this treasure was subsequently distributed among them. For a long time afterwards, however, stray pieces of these antique coins continued to be surreptitiously sold in Sidon, so that doubtless the whole treasure was not given up by the peasants. They were all gold coins of Philip of Macedon and of Alexander the Great, of the most beautiful workmanship, the latter appearing as if they had been just struck from the mint.

It can be readily appreciated that to any one of that poverty-stricken band the disparity between the worth of the least of these gold pieces and the utmost reward of his daily toil would make him willing to part with all his worldly goods, if so he could gain that treasure.

The land of the parables is, in fact, undoubtedly full of such buried treasures, for scarce a year passed of my residence there in which I did not hear of such discoveries. Once I bought several silver coins of the Seleucidæ of Antioch from a considerable collection of them which some children found shining in a mole-hill near a village of Upper Galilee, and on another occasion, not a hundred yards from our house in Sidon, a soldier found an earthen jar full of old Turkish gold coins, which were struck by the early sultans before Turkish money had become debased. The reason for these frequent discoveries is not far to seek. For more than forty centuries it has been a common practice with the inhabitants of that country to bury their silver and their gold whenever a war or an oppressor threatened them with the loss of all they had; and when we consider how often in the history of that land cities and towns have been captured, and the inhabitants either all massacred or sold as slaves, it is no wonder that the secret of such hidden treasures in multitudes of instances perished with those who buried them. Such hiding of silver and of gold, I knew, was still going on when I lived there by native Christian merchants, on the oft-recurring fears of massacres by their Moslem neighbors, and with good reason, as the terrible slaughter of the Christians in Damascus in 1860 proved. There being no way open in former times of transferring valuables from one country to another, the silent bosom of mother earth thus has ever been the one receptacle thought of by the Oriental for safe keeping. In many instances government officials or rulers have similarly buried vast treasures.* From the fact that this large sum of Macedonian gold found in Sidon was exclusively made up of fresh coins, those of Alexander apparently having never been used, it is very probable that the leaden boxes were deposited where they were found by some embezzler among Alexander's own army officials while that monarch was residing in Sidon, when he was conducting the siege of Tyre. So settled was this practice even in Phœnician times that every inscription yet found on the sarcophagi of Phœnician kings consists chiefly of earnest adjurations to treasure-seekers not to disturb their rest, because they would find no valuables within.

---

* In the *Reminiscences of the Great Mutiny*, by W. Forbes Mitchell, p. 152, is given a graphic account of the labors of the soldiers of the 93d Highlanders, with other detachments, in raising, from a well at Poona, boxes containing money valued at £306,250, besides plate and other valuables said to be worth more than a million sterling, which had been secreted there by Nana Sahib in his flight from Cawnpore.

When, here in America, the legend of a noted buccaneer of the eighteenth century, named Captain Kidd, having buried a treasure of Spanish gold somewhere between points a thousand miles apart along our Atlantic coast, has led to numerous attempts to find it, we need not wonder that in Syria every inhabitant has hopes that ere he dies he shall become boundlessly enriched by such a secret gift of fortune. Tales of the kind excite the imagination of every child in that land, and they continue to cherish them throughout life. Scarcely does a man indulge in an unusual outlay or expense but his neighbors begin to rally him with questions whether he has come upon some golden store in a field or well.

It is this wide-spread and well-founded belief that there are buried treasures of untold value all over the land which furnishes the special parallel to a great truth about Christ and men in this world. Instead of a surprise undreamt of, as a treasure-trove would be to a man in this country, this parable is based upon a most familiar idea to dwellers in Palestine, of riches heard of throughout their lives, and whose discovery is constantly hoped for. But are not the riches of Christ and the kingdom of heaven widely known and spoken of among us? Yet nothing is truer than that the world does not see them, but ever leaves them to become matters of personal discovery.

It is well to ponder why this is so. In no other religion is there anything which corresponds to this finding of Christ by the Christian. In a Mohammedan country all men hear about Mohammed, just as in a Christian country all men hear about Christ; but does a Moslem ever need to "find" Mohammed? And yet, though multitudes have been told from their childhood, often most earnestly by their own parents, what an inestimable gift from God is Christ, nevertheless, in an important sense, he always remains hidden, and a treasure to be found. To the end of time this seeming paradox of the parable will hold true. Neither the hearing of the ear, nor the reasoning of the mind, nor any enumeration of the "evidences of Christianity" will change the fact that the true revelation of Christ to a man is ever a new as well as a most critical event in his life.

The great difference among men in their estimation of Christ is solely due to this fact. To some he is their all in all, practically dominating their every object and choice in life. Their devotion to him is such that they are ready to surrender for his sake all that men naturally would hold to the last. Whenever the test has come, life itself has not been too precious to be refused by the Christian for his Lord. But all this is as inexplicable to the men of the world as the action of a man who would exchange his whole property for a small, barren-looking field. Most men of the world, indeed, secretly regard Christians as deluded visionaries. And so they are unless Christ be an infinitely greater treasure than all the treasures together of this world. But if he be of such transcendent worth, why is he to the world as gold buried out of sight?

We need not feel this to be a difficulty when we consider that it is not the knowledge of Christ only which is similarly hidden from men. Other momentous facts which concern all men without exception appear to be just as strangely buried out of their sight. Thus if there be any certainty on earth, it is that death awaits every one born into this world; and yet who does not act as if practically he felt that he need not take death into account? So strong is this confidence in one's own immortality here, so to speak, that in war men can always be found to lead a forlorn hope more from a feeling that others are to fall and not they than from any deliberate calculation of the risk to be run. We do not even find advancing age, with its clear demonstration that the end cannot be far off, yet bring the grave any nearer to view, for men then still behave as if it were as distant to them as ever. Old men are as ready as any younger men to build houses which they cannot long occupy, or to plant trees whose fruit they can scarcely expect to gather.

Now it is a mistake to say that this is because men cling to life. It is not because they cling to life, but because they forget death. It is because the other world, and everything which concerns it, even the portal of its entrance, are so wholly hidden from men's minds by this present world that no thoughts but those which go below the surface of their daily lives will ever awaken them to the importance of the hereafter, and thus to the supreme importance of Christ.

It is, therefore, a great thing for a man to find his thoughts awakening to the weighty subject of the End. It is then that he has begun to tread a field where a great treasure can be found. For it is impossible to appreciate the full significance of death to us here without soon recognizing what a sad orphanage human life without God is on this earth. The one word which best comports with the facts of man's earthly existence is—insecurity. Made to enjoy and to love many things, not one of them can he be sure of for a day. Years make every one more and more a loser, and if he attain to old age, what has he attained to then but to a wreck of his former self. Finally, he is told by the world that the debt of Nature has to be paid. Need we wonder, in view of what that last payment is, often after so many other heavy payments, that many wish the debt had never been incurred? It is a pathetic illustration of the underlying sense of their orphanage, that so many millions of our race have accepted the teaching of the Gautama Buddha that all conscious existence is a punishment, and that the best thing which can come to a good man is an eternal sleep! But to every heart burdened with earth's dark destiny and darker ending comes the word of this parable, joined with that former gracious injunction, "Seek, and ye shall find." Not a heavenly kingdom on earth, which therefore must perish with all earthly things, but ye shall find the Kingdom of Heaven, where the Father waits the coming of his child. When that is found, all the weight of man's helplessness here, and of life's long poverty, vanishes. Naked we came into this world, but the finding of this treasure insures our leaving it rich indeed with an eternal possession which cannot be spent; for it is not the pay of the hireling who barely lives by paying it out again. The man who finds a hid treasure has not received it in payment, nor could he ever have earned a tithe of its value by his own exertions. So he who works on earth even for a heavenly reward, will be paid only according to the wages of earth, and in its poor coin, without receiving one of the golden pieces of God's great treasure. As unfamiliar to him at first as were the shining ancient coins to the eyes of the poor Sidon peasants, he who begins to take the full measure of this treasure of the parable which so long has been waiting for him learns more and more of its inestimable worth, though he may not be able to reveal it to the world, and only carry the full knowledge of it as his own secret. But this he knows, that its revelation of a loving fellowship with God, cemented by Christ, and furnished for every step of his sojourn here, exchanges the sense of life's loneliness for the sanctifying sense of a sacred companionship which shall not end until, with all who are made pure in heart, he shall see God!

THE PEARL

Matt. xiii., 45, 46.

Again, the kingdom of heaven is like unto a merchantman, seeking goodly pearls: Who, when he had found one pearl of great price, went and sold all that he had, and bought it.

THE PEARL

A PEARL of the first quality is unquestionably the most beautiful object in nature. However brilliant the hard and cold diamond may be, yet it cannot approach in loveliness the bright but delicate lustre of the pearl. Moreover, as an authority on the subject remarks, "of all the objects employed as ornaments, the pearl is almost the only one which derives nothing from art. On the contrary, all attempts to give it more value only end in deteriorating it."* Its worth, therefore, is always intrinsic, and wholly dependent upon its own properties. Hence the very great difference between pearls. There are natural pearls of a beautiful form and ample size, which, however, do not display those wonderful reflections of white light mingled with azure which command a great price. They

* *A Popular Account of Gems*, by Louis Dieulafait, p. 192, Scribner.

are, therefore, called dead pearls, and may be very cheaply bought. In all ages the pearl really possessing the purest tints outranks in costliness all except a very few diamonds. Julius Cæsar gave one such to Servilia, the sister of Cato, for which he paid a sum equal to $223,000 of our money. A jewel which cost but one-thousandth of this amount would generally be considered expensive, but so rare and yet unmistakable is the highest quality of these exquisite objects that history abounds with statements of still more extraordinary sums which have been paid for single pearls. We should not fail to note, therefore, that when such a pearl is found by the seeker, he knows that only in the highest quarters should he offer it. "One famous pearl was brought from the Indies by Gorgibus of Calais, and presented to Philip IV. of Spain. 'How have you ventured,' asked Philip of the merchant, 'to put all your fortune into such a little object?' 'I knew there was in the world the king of Spain to buy it of me,' the merchant answered. There was but one royal way of rewarding such faith as this, and Philip IV.

became forthwith the owner of the pearl of Gorgibus."*

Special knowledge, indeed, of the highest order is requisite on the part of a pearl merchant. Only long acquaintance with the respective merits of thousands of specimens would fit him safely to put all his fortune into one 'such little object,' knowing that by doing so he was making a very great gain. But both in ancient times and in the Orient to this day the search of a merchant for goodly pearls is one which commonly entails much personal hardship and danger. Whether on the shores of the Red Sea or of the Persian Gulf, where the pearls are obtained from the fishermen, those regions have always had an evil repute for the character of their inhabitants. Even in Bagdad or in Damascus, the life of a man known to be carrying a pearl of great price about him would not be safe for an hour. Often, therefore, these possessors of costly pearls disguise themselves and accompany caravans as poor religious beggars or pilgrims, while they

---

* *A Popular Account of Gems*, by Louis Dieulafait, p. 196, Scribner.

may have secreted in their bosoms more than what would buy all the goods of their companions. We need not wonder, therefore, that the man himself becomes an enthusiast over the preciousness of his treasure. His whole life is bound up in it. His one sole restorative, through the long desert journey, is secretly now and then to feast his eyes upon its matchless beauty, while he thinks of the hour when it shall give him entrance into the presence of the king.

The difference between the parables of the hid treasure and the pearl is that the finding of the treasure might occur to any one, though in fact it usually comes to a poor working-man while engaged in his ordinary daily toil, and because he happened to be so engaged. The pearl merchant, on the other hand, devotes himself to a definite search, for which he has undergone a long training, so that he can appreciate the different values between pearls, while he never ceases to hope that he will yet gain possession of some unequalled prize which will crown the labor of his life. Frequent are the parallels to such a seeker in the story of the Church of God of pure and noble spirits who by nature were inclined to be ever looking for the goodly pearls of truth just for their own sake. In the search for wisdom and knowledge there are many such pearls to be found whose value is great, and it testifies to a high instinct in a man for him to choose any such pursuit. The precious pearl of the parable does not preclude there being in the world many other beautiful and costly gems which are worth seeking and possessing. It only enjoins the search for the one pearl which will be worth presenting to the king, and it implies that the knowledge of all true pearls, instead of hindering, will rather assist the more in finding this greatest of them all.

The memory of one such seeker, Justin Martyr, should ever be cherished by the Church with especial affection as the forerunner of many who through the ages have witnessed to the prophecy of this parable by letting the world know why, after much seeking, they found no preciousness like the preciousness of Christ. At this very day the testimony of Justin is fought over between the friends and the foes of Christianity, from a clear recognition of its historical importance. In his Dialogue Justin tells his own story with that simple sincerity which gives the true strain of his nature, for he wrote with a perfect knowledge that it might bring death to him, as in fact it did. Justin began as a searcher for truth among the old philosophic schools. He applied first to a Stoic, then to an Aristotelian peripatetic, then to a Pythagorean, and then to a Platonist. With this last teacher he seemed to himself to grow wiser every day. It was at that time, " when," as he says, " in my folly I hoped soon to attain to a clearer vision of God, that, seeking calm and retirement by the sea-shore, I met an aged man, meek and venerable, who led me at length from philosophy and metaphysics to faith. 'Pray before all things,' were the last words of this new master, 'that the gates of light be opened to you.' Immediately" (after prayer), Justin adds, "a fire was kindled in my soul, and as I discussed his arguments with myself, I found Christianity to be the only philosophy that is sure, and suited to man's wants. Thus, then, and for this cause, am I a philosopher."

It was a dangerous thing at that time for a man like Justin to let it be known that he had come upon such a discovery. It meant that he should be ready for it to give up everything—name, philosophy, life. But ready to exchange all these, he came forward to address Marcus Aurelius in defence of Christ and his cause, appealing as a philosopher to a philosopher. The result was that the philosophic Aurelius became all the more determined that he who claimed the right as a philosopher to advocate the cause of the despised Galilean should pay for it with his blood. Need we doubt that Justin now found his pearl steadily gain in its sweet lustre, till from his prison he went forth to kneel at the block? A short moment there, and he passed to give his one treasure to Him who alone could own it. For now the splendid pearl is seen to be the man himself, reflecting in his perfected spirit all the glory of Heaven's pure light. The treasures of wisdom and of knowledge which the world prizes so much God does not need, for He has them all and more. But what he has long and ever desired is the possession of just such sons of men. "And they shall be mine, saith the Lord of hosts, in that day when I make up my jewels." (Malachi iii. 17, rendered in the Revised Version, "a peculiar treasure.")

Everything in the preceding parables leads up to this pair of the hid treasure and of the pearl as the crowning teaching of them all. A wide field of thought intervenes between the conception of the seed of the first parable and the pearl of great price, for we come to the inmost heart of the truth about the kingdom when it is presented as a single object of inestimable worth which is only found by a man for himself. The teaching of the hid treasure and of the pearl, therefore, refers to a deeply personal relation of the kingdom, which from its very nature cannot be spoken about always and everywhere. Our Lord indeed had enjoined before a wise form of Christian reticence, which by some is too often forgotten, when he said, "Cast not your pearls before swine." So there is a sacred truth about Christ and each believer which the world can neither see nor appreciate, but which is the one explanation of Christ's enduring hold upon men from age to age. It is this which sustains his follower just when he has to go, as all others have to go, alone to the grave. The difference between the Christian and all others, then, is this pearl, or the knowledge that Jesus is his own divine redeemer. If Jesus be only a man there would be no room in him for that knowledge of every individual heart which the Christian is taught to depend upon. No finite being, though an archangel, could ever fill the place of Christ at death, because for that great hour of individual experience the human heart can accept nothing less than God, that blessed Infinite One who alone can be to each man as if he were the only one of his children. The mysterious union of each of his people to Christ, of which the New Testament speaks, becomes, therefore, an intelligible doctrine when the truth about the Son of God is known. To feel that he knows all about us as God only can know—our longings and our fears, and everything which our spirits would express, but for weakness cannot—and that he will supply out of his divine love whatever we lack, making us rich indeed, now, at death, and forever, is that personal revelation in the kingdom of heaven whose preciousness cannot be told in words. That Jesus died for every man is a doctrine which implies that he could do so as an actual fact, and not in a general or representative sense. It is this conviction which consecrates every life so bought to a complete heart service in life to Him who thus has become the dearest of friends, our helper in every need and difficulty, whether without or within, even to the hour when his shepherd form will be seen going before, as we follow into the Valley of the Shadow of Death.

THE HOUSEHOLDER'S TREASURE

Matt. xiii., 51, 52.

Jesus saith unto them, Have ye understood all these things? They say unto him, Yea, Lord. Then said he unto them, Therefore every scribe which is *instructed unto the kingdom of heaven, is like unto a man* that is *a householder, which bringeth forth out of his treasure* things new and old.

THE HOUSEHOLDER'S TREASURE

The close of our Lord's teaching on that eventful day at the Lake was with an illustration given to his disciples of the varied aspects and many-sidedness of the kingdom which he was to establish through them upon the earth. At present, as in that age, the distribution of wealth in Palestine is so unequal that the difference is wide indeed between the common man, whose shelf shows only a few vessels of clay, and whose coat is his one covering at night (Exod. xxii. 27), and the "son of men," as the Arabic term is for those who correspond to the "householders" of the parables. During my own young days we spent the summer months at Mount Lebanon villages in the ordinary houses of the people, where, among other signs of the same poverty as in old times, the infants are still not uncommonly laid during the daytime in the mangers of the cattle. Such an experience makes one appreciate how our modern manufactures have enriched the homes of our poor with many an article, from a glass tumbler to a clock, which even the rich could not show in former times. But in contrast with our cheaply-turned-out fineries, the store of a wealthy emir may abound with treasures which no machine can duplicate, precious in material, and still more in the art and skill which wrought them. Among these would be cashmere shawls, embroideries in cloth and leather, splendid vessels of silver and of gold; inlaid armor and jewelled sword-hilts, with blades whose steel is the despair of modern metal-workers. These are his things old, shown with a just historic pride, and not old in the sense that such a man would keep in his store anything worn out. Rather that which he would show as new acquisitions would have to be of much intrinsic value, so as to correspond with the high worth of the old.

This illustration of the householder was based upon the examples which our Lord had just given how the one theme of the kingdom afforded many great themes of varied interest and of supreme importance. Always will there be many precious things old and precious things new to offer to this poor world about the kingdom of God. With such a subject a Christian teacher has no excuse for sameness or dulness, and should be the last man to be charged with a poverty of ideas. Also he should no more dwell monotonously on some one truth out of the rest of his rich store than the householder would bring forth but one of his treasures as if that were all. Such a phrase as "preaching the simple Gospel" should never imply that the Gospel itself is simple, for it is very much the reverse, and so infinitely varied in its relations to the hearts of men that no man can preach it truthfully by merely repeating the words of another man, even though an inspired man. He must instead give something of the newness of his own spirit and feeling to illustrate whatever precious old truths it affords him, for God has not made men duplicates in their hearts or in their experiences any more than in their features or their voices. Each generation, also, is a new generation, and a preacher should show that he is a man of his time as well as one well furnished with the rich heritage of former generations.

CONCLUSION

CONCLUSION

We may say, in conclusion, that in one great respect the parables are a special revelation of Christ himself. An illustration always implies something very definite in the mind beforehand which is to be illustrated, and hence from these parables we deduce the central conception itself which Jesus had from the beginning. Pervading them all, and unifying them as parts of one whole, is his Kingdom of Heaven. Much of the significance of the parables, however, the men of that day could not enter into because they were prophecies, whose coming true we can perceive now, but which then required generations yet unborn to prove. Jesus looked far beyond the multitude standing before him to scenes and events of a very distant future. He foretold that the kingdom which was then the least of all the seeds would wax so great that his and its natural foes, even the very children of Satan, would fain ally themselves with it for their own purposes. This kind of success would never have occurred to human imagination, but history answers with such spectacles as the Cæsar entering the fold from motives of worldly calculation, and after him more than one great monarch compelled to fall at the feet of men who claimed all power on earth because they were the successors of one of those fishermen of that day on the Lake. Though happily such forms of fulfilment of the parables of the tares and of the draw-net cannot recur now that the worldly attractions of the Church are lessening, yet it remains true that no men, whether Jews or not, would have pictured a coming kingdom other than with the old bodily sway of a political dominion, without the faintest conception of that mightier rule over the spirits as well as the bodies of men which Jesus knew that his kingdom would wield even when perverted.

These aspects of the kingdom, however, are but its incidental historical accompaniments. Above all and through all runs the great truth that his kingdom, though in this world, is not of this world, but of heaven. This conception was too high not only for the Galilean multitude, but for other multitudes as well, down to our own day. There are some among us who fondly cherish an ideal which is virtually the same as that of the ancient Jews, of a kingdom which Christ will establish at his Second Advent, when he will personally reign in the city of Jerusalem. But one would suppose that even in the days of Jewish expectancy some thoughtful minds would have asked, of what abiding worth can any earthly kingdom, even the Messiah's, be to men, when at best they could enjoy its benefits only for the brief period of their natural lives? Without death being abolished, along with disease and suffering, without the whole present economy of nature being entirely changed, how could men have but a life interest, so to speak, in such an estate? But if such a change should occur, of what service would an earthly Jerusalem be then for the many millions of the human race of any generation, not to mention all the redeemed of every generation, a multitude we are told which no man can number? The entire area of the Jerusalem which our Lord visited does not equal the area of the Central Park of New York. Such a fact shows how easily the imagination can emancipate itself from all reasoning when it turns to dreaming about the Lord's kingdom.

Moreover, the conceptions of many minds about the future triumph of the Church on earth are bound with much the same sort of secular limitations; for they plainly think more of her restoration to full power in this present world than of her connection with the world to come. But are the Christians of the future, or of the millennium, to possess a greater importance in the kingdom than we do, or than those who have preceded us in the faith? After all is said about the importance of the visible Church on earth, how can she for a moment compare in true personal interest for every one with the Church in heaven? It would be well for any one who sets such store upon the particular church "pale" in which he is found to reflect how he may meet at the King's right hand with his chosen ones out of another fold. Of what importance will it then seem to which temporary fold on earth the heirs of the everlasting Kingdom of Heaven belonged?

In completest contrast with all such passing things as any and every kingdom which men conceive of, spoke in the parables He whose words shall not pass away, though the heavens and the earth shall pass away. Here he tells us that man is not a temporary being, because he belongs to a kingdom which shall have no end. There is, and there always has been, a thing permanent in man, and that is religion. The forms in which this element in his nature has manifested itself have constantly varied, changed, and passed away, but his interest in religion itself has remained unchanged and unchangeable, as it ever seeks to find its last and abiding resting-place. In these parables our Lord foretold the story of long ages to come because he knew that he was dealing with a permanent force in human nature which comes from man's intuition that there is more than this world which he sees about him, and a life more enduring than that which his fleeting breath sustains. This old witness to the Kingdom of Heaven our Lord appealed to when he exclaimed, "He who hath ears to hear, let him hear!" for men always have been conscious of a higher, purer, better life than they find anywhere in this world. In proportion to their longing for such a world would their hearts be natural, honest, and good, and thus ready to receive the seed-beginning of its life from Him who is its divine sower. That seed would manifest itself first in the field of earthly life where it was sown, in bringing forth the fruits of righteousness, peace, and all goodness, until this world itself would become transformed and changed by the mighty but silent working of this heaven-sent life. Do not the mind and the heart both answer that his words must be true, for how else can a life in heaven be possible? Without a nature purified from every trace of that love of self which is the source of all sin, immortality, with its inconceivable opportunities for action, would be only an awful curse. But with a perfect transformation into the likeness of the King himself, whose name is the Lamb of Sacrifice, entitling the changed man then to society with him and with all the sons of God, our Lord's revelation of such a Kingdom of Heaven makes it meet indeed to exchange all this poor world can give for its priceless and beautiful inheritance.

THE END

www.ingramcontent.com/pod-product-compliance
Lightning Source LLC
Chambersburg PA
CBHW030248170426
43202CB00009B/668